Table of Contents
Turn to next page

Author of: Not Forbidden-Your Oral Delight (same book)
   Mz. Jee's Spot aka Annjee Your Love/Relationship Specialist
Illustrator: Leon
Editors: Alex L. , V. Hes / Final Edit completed by Patti M.
Published in the USA
Printed by: Everything & More Company
everythingandmore@sbcglobal.net
Copyright ©2010 by Village Sista Girlfriend Series
©# Txu-1-688-418
ISBN # 978-0-9833491-0-5
Cover and Inside revised: 2012
Trademark Registration V.S.G. -Village Sista Girlfriend
Pending

Visit: www.VSGseries.com
for products, resources and information
Facebook: Village Sista Girlfriend (V.S.G)
Twitter: @VSG__Angie or @VSG_Jee
Email: vsgseries@yahoo.com

This book or any other materials from Village Sista Girlfriend or Everything and More Co can not be reprinted, copied and duplicated in any form unless, a written permit is issued and signed by author or owner. Thank you

Thank YOU - Share this information

Village Sista Girlfriend
V.S.G. SERIES

*Great Manuel for Love Classes
ask Your Specialist about it*

The *Women's Guide* to Steppin Out of Your Box and getting an **A+** in the Highest Learning of your man

Have fun and reread the book. We will talk on Facebook, emails, Twitter, or on the phone. Just have a Ladies Nite Out event/retreat and call me! Polls, Blogs and Forums online This is the same as the book Not Forbidden - Your Oral Delight

After you finish reading the book, talk about it to everyone you know. I love the interesting feed back and debates I've had with men and women about the book. Share the knowledge; recommend this book to friends. Host a Ladies Nite Party with your girls. Have your Toy Specialist educate you about romantic goodies and learn even more exciting ways to love and be loved better.

SCAN for Deals on Books, Parties and Classes

Thank YOU — Scan Codes and forward to friends

For ALL the Ladies - Share this information

Bring Out **V.S.G. SERIES** *Your ORAL DIVA*

Sista - is a term used to describe another sister from another motha, bearing no blood relation, but you love her just the same, for she is now a part of your circle of friends and family.

We are ALL *Sistas(ers)* related by the most powerful man controlling, thing known in the entire world... Our Minds and the power of the Almighty Vagina. No matter what age, race, status, creed or religion, the problems are the same between us. Everyone need solutions, motivation, someone to talk to, be heard by and a non judgmental sista that has been in your shoes. What's most important, (I feel) is I am not afraid to admit it and want to share the myths, lies, solutions and Awesome techniques I've learned and tried over the years.
Tabooish topics like this really doesn't exit, unless YOU say they do! So I welcome you to the Deprogramming and Re-Education of your past and on to a more powerful and confident you.

What is the Village, Sista, Girlfriend's Philosophy

<u>Count forward to Page 7 (gray pages)
in the introduction section</u>
to know exactly the unity between us and get on board with the plan...
Getting an A+ in the Highest Learning of Your Man

Hello My Sista from   Mz. Jee's Spot

For MORE FUN, have a PARTY or CLASS

Has the LOVE Game Changed?

Love is not hard,
but deprogramming yourself can be;
especially, if you do it alone.
You must realize old habits and outdated concepts will produce the same results and outcome that you are probably tired of.

The world hasn't changed, but the game of love has. What was once taboo [oral sex], has been shamefully and secretly done since the beginning of time. Now, oral sex, is an enjoyable requirement in a relationship. The fear and mis-education of many sistas has society thinking that ALL men are dogs. Not True!

More times then not, *we* give our man to the other woman on a tempting plate filled with strawberries & whip crème on top and never realize how.
Read the Village Sist Girlfriend Series to understand how this happens and how you can prevent it.

Your
Love & Relationship
Specialist:
Mz. Jee's Spot

Don't Suck at Suckin

That is sooooo, not sexy
Your man will appreciate you for this

SO PLEASE
Read the book in its entirety.

You cannot learn to be good if you are skipping pages, flickering through the book for the pictures and *good* stuff.
It's ALL Good
when you understand why you are uncomfortable with it from the start.

The How To's, Assignments and Homework will be a lot easier to do if you understand your dilemma.

Visit us online www.VSGseries.com

V.S.G. series

Thank You

This book could not have been created if it weren't for Leon, my illustrator buddy. He can draw *erthing*. Sheer professional talent was bestowed upon him thru his maker and his *'Yo Go Baby'* wife. You guys are a marital inspiration. Thanks (thks) again.

OMG! My girl, Mz. Alex L, (first editor) was introduced to me by fate (thks Mz. Monica). In an idol conversation, we started talking about our dreams of self employment and writing. I told her what I was doing... we think alike, I jumped at the opportunity to put the book in her hands. She captured my essence. Only she could do that. Thks. To Patti M (final editor) this could not have happened w/o You. Thks

The encouraging words and search for people who could help me with the book was priceless. I will always be in touch, no matter what. Thks Mz. Tammy. Amy, & Nick for all the help and for just being YOU - YOUS GUYS

To all my *Hen Party* sistas, family and friends. You gave me the most encouraging words on such a tabooish topic. To all my *Got Yo Back Buddies*. Even my mom was on board with this (love U ma). V Hess, you gave insight that I couldn't have gotten from any other source - homies for life. Man, Candy you were the missing piece to my book puzzle. You always come thru. To Mrs. B.O, A.V, Y.A, Mz. A.P and A.H thks for being my comical village, sistas and girlfriends. Great minds think alike. For the ones who donated before the book was even completed - Thank you for your trust. Donations are always welcome. This won't be the last book, so donations and speaking engagements are needed.

<u>Tell everyone you know about The *V.S.G.* Series</u>

Call Me for your next Ladies Event * Book Club Reading * Couples Retreat * or just because

Thank YOU — Scan Codes and forward to friends

Bring Out

Your ORAL DIVA

You are a part of our Village.
Write the information of the person who's (place card below)
responsible for you purchasing the book
You will always be able to contact each other

Place person's information/card here

For MORE FUN, have a PARTY or CLASS

The V.S.G. series

What is the Village, Sista, Girlfriend's Philosophy

Welcome to our *Village* - Being a part of a village is not just for our children, it's for all who believe in love, guidance, a helping hand and realize that educating themselves is a never ending journey.

We are now *Sistas* - Sista is not a black thing. It's a word you use when you are comfortable enough to talk about everything to a woman who's not related by blood, but by the laughter, love, sweat and tears we share as all of us go thru the trials and tribulations of life. As you read this book, you will find you are not alone. The topics that I address are common situations that so many women need help with. A sista such as yourself, is always just a click away from another sista with the same dilemma(s). We can talk and listen to each another when advice is needed or when just wanting to give a testimony. I am your sista, we come from similar places - with the goal of wanting to be a better woman, lover, mother and friend.

So, if you don't want to lose great guys over fixable things, be single forever, and/or never break the cycle of dating the wrong men – then let this sista share all the information from the other women, my own experience and things men have shared with me about loving sistas. The things men truly want in relationships, *statistical polls* just doesn't cut it nor does it dig deep enough to add beneficial insight to

purpose of this book

Re-Education and Deprogramming starts Here
www.VSGseries.com

some of the real dilemmas in relationships the average person can relate to.

As your *Girlfriend* - We can get downright dirty and nasty and talk about all the things our parents and society told us not to talk about. We can bring out the freak in each other and not feel guilty learning how to love and be loved better. We can keep each other rational during those irrational times. And I'm one girlfriend that don't want your man, but instead, want to make you the bestest partner, the bestest friend, and the bestest fuck your man has ever had. As your girl, you can ask me anything. There's no such thing as a silly or inappropriate question that shouldn't be asked or answered from either of us.

Only your girlfriend can make you feel good during some of the worst of times - I hope, I can be that friend for you. And just like that girlfriend you've known most of your life, you will probably get mad at some of the things I might write about or say. And as sistas often do, we might not agree about some things, but whatever I say or write about is out of love.

So far, I haven't heard any new problems, dilemmas, new scenarios about relationships or our inner struggles and men. Sometimes the truth hurts - but will set you free, if you let it.
Sincerely Genuine,

Mz. Jee's Spot, The Village Sista Girlfriend

purpose of this book

To The Man Above and the One I Look Up To

Thank you for making me comfortable enough to hear you say
OOOOH GOD!!!

I appreciate the support I've gotten from my *Hen Party Sistas* over the years. You have helped make me a better woman, wife, lover, teacher, listener, and friend to my huzband. And as a result of being and feeling better, I am also better to you. I've been blessed with a sexy and encouraging huzband who's understandably eager to help me in my many V.S.G. plights in every way imaginable. He goes out of his way to help me help all sistas suffering from Oral Sex dilemmas to overcome their fears.

He wanted me to tell all sistas...
"If you think the key to a man's heart is thru his stomach - **you're aiming too high."**

You encourage me to practice on you continuously. You insist that I incorporate new techniques as you've single handedly helped me master my Oral Sex skillz. We are a young couple, sixteen years strong and counting. I love you.

Thank You, Sweetie.
For being my trainer, man and fan.

P.S. We were having Oral Sex *before* we said "I Do." He was HP (Husband Potential) and I was WP (Wife Potential) *before* the *I Do's*. Stop using marriage as your crutch, especially when you are doing everything ELSE.

#1 RULE - ONLY *select* and get involved with the type of man that has the potential to be your huzband!

About the Author

Hello my V.S.G. Sista

If you are wondering why I did a cartoon version of me versus a portrait, it's simple; I enjoy my privacy as you are entitled to yours. I see sistas all the time who have been to many things I've hosted, and as we say Hi and talk to each other, we become a part of each other's village. I enjoy being accessible to my sistas and brothas. Trust me, I plan on sharing the V.S.G. Philosophy with everyone. I hope you will join me in getting the word out.

Love

Mz. Jee's Spot aka Angie, Your Love Specialist

 Homework/Assignments - Should be completed before you go to the next page.

 **The gray** squares and oval shapes are filled with information that is a cliff note to what you should remember, if nothing else.

 Other boxes have interesting facts and things can that can make you say hmmm.

A+ in the Highest Learning of Your Man
www.VSGseries.com

Sorry, no long introduction here

Most sistas don't have time for themselves and are unable to read a book in peace without the read being interrupted by someone or something. This book is equivalent to sneaking and reading your mother's XXX rated *'How To'* books. You really wanted to read the books, you were so curious, but you were conflicted. You were taught since birth that the type of stuff you found in your parents room was nasty and bad for you. If you didn't find them, they just hid them well.

Although you are grown now and searching for answers to better yourself, you still feel guilty. You're not sure if you should even continue to read this after this paragraph because you don't want anyone to know you're reading this type of book. You can't see the

Ask your Specialist about Classes & Products

benefits right now, but in the end, you will be more comfortable with the act of Oral Sex and satisfying your partner.

Let me ease your mind a little. First, your man has been wishing that you read this book a long time ago. And it's not because he thinks that you are bad at Oral Sex, but it makes him feel good knowing that you cared enough about him and his needs to go out of your comfort zone and do something that is truly not about degrading you, It is simply a sexual act, like any other sexual position/act that the two of you do to, for and with each other.

Be proud of yourself! You took the initiative to seek new knowledge and try to make a change in your relationship. Just like your mother's sex/lovemaking books you stumbled across when you were young, get excited about creating your own collection! The difference is, you can get excited about using this knowledge; *it's guilt free*! You don't have to be alone trying to solve dilemmas about your sex life, as your mother probably had to do. I'm here to help you every step of the way. You can always email me or chat on the blog with myself and others just like us.

Our mothers didn't have the support or the encouraging words to jump right into changing their *good girl* syndrome. As a result, many of our mother's sexual hang ups remained, leaving a bottomless pit of unhappiness in potentially good relationships with the men in their lives.

Even today, Oral Sex continues to be a touchy subject. I wasn't raised to feel comfortable about Oral Sex either, so I can relate with what you're going through. Many women of all ages and nationalities are looking for the same answers. That is why I write to you as the Village Sista Girlfriend.

I am not going to drown you with unnecessary medical terminology or perfectly correct English - if you are in need of all that...

"I Ain't the One!"

BUT if you need real–life perspectives from a sista who's not ashamed to confess to not being with many men *(I believe in quality over quantity),* and believe in selecting a brotha with huzband potential versus being a friend with benefits, this can be a beneficial read to you. I have helped many men and women on this topic, not to mention many years of my own personal doctorish research that consisted of personal guinea pig moments on my man (my huzband) and my many awakening moments about my own upbringing.

Ask your Specialist about Classes & Products

> My parents raised me with the best intentions. SO IF you are looking to do a blow job like a porn star, want to learn how to suck off a group of brothas or you must receive advice from a professional hoodrat or mistress, then this book might not be for you.

This book is small enough to fit in your purse, so always keep it with you. When you have to run errands or wait for the kids at basketball practice, and you find yourself with moments to spare, take the initiative to devote some quality time and complete some of the Self Help section.

Read the book wherever, people won't have a clue what you are reading - except another Village Sista Girlfriend reader seeking the same knowledge. Ultimately, I hope in time, you will learn not to give a damn about what others think when it comes to what is in the best interest for your relationship. AND! eventually, break the cycle and share this book and knowledge with other sistas, unlike the secrecy our mothers had to go through.

A+ in the Highest Learning of Your Man
www.VSGseries.com

SOOOOOO

Carve a little time for yourself. Take a bath, close the door and create a little sanctuary for yourself and read the book

This book belongs to

_____

The Pledge

I am preparing myself for the opportunity to change. It is my duty to treat this book like a journal. I will take note of things that will improve my relationship versus a secret diary concealing my fears.

I must put forth the effort to improve, listen and remain open minded as I look into to my soul, my past, and my future in order to better understand who I am today, how I got here and learning to rejoice being a new reinvented me tomorrow.

CHAPTER 1

Why I Wrote This Book

Plain and simple, Oral Sex has gotten a bad rap! From infancy to death, a sista is never made to feel good about giving head. And from infancy to death, a brotha is obsessed with touching his penis until he realizes that it feels even better when someone else touches it. He is forever hooked, at whatever age, when he *finds* someone that will put their warm moist mouth on it... IF The Experience WAS Good! OMG! Get ready to be in constant conflict with your man and this oral sex thing. And, even if it was bad... OMG! He still wants it and you and your man will *still* be in constant conflict over the oral sex thing.

If you are like how I *use* to be, a sista that picked up on all the words versus the message, you might have turned your lips up, in confirmation, to the words "when he *finds* someone" and "*still* be in constant conflict with your man." Your confirmation is probably negative as to why you shouldn't do it. Words like *find* and *still* told me that a man doesn't care who gives him head and *still,* meant to

Conflicted

me, that no matter what I did, he wouldn't be satisfied—so why do it at all! The conflict is understandable. Ask yourself -**Who do you think about when you hear the words oral sex/giving head?**

1. _____   2. _____

3. _____   4. _____

If you are like how I use to be, you probably have negative thoughts and wrote words like: sluts, freaks, hoes, hoodrats, busdowns, nasty or gross. When I associated oral sex/giving head with the words above, I too, was conflicted. I was raised to be a good girl and me and freaks and hoes weren't on the same level (you will read scenarios about how this affects you later). So I was resistant to doing that oral thing on my man for many years. I thought that way up until my mid twenties.

I reprogrammed myself, but it took years without help. You don't have to find or luck up on the answers; many answers are in this book and the rest we can discover as a village. Instead of always searching for the words to make me not wanna do it or instead of zoning in on the *find* and the negativity, I realized *find* didn't mean just anyone because I didn't let just *anyone,* go down on me. Most importantly, I didn't just let *anyone* in my life, to love me. And I never selected a brotha who just dated *anyone,* before he met me.

Chapter 1   **WHY ME...**

That thought process set me apart from all the rats and sluts. I knew I wasn't any of those sistas and I couldn't continue to use that as one of the excuses not to give my man oral pleasure.

My heart and reprogramming made me change my old state of mind. I couldn't continue to justify my selfish ways by denying my man pleasures that I enjoyed also; simply because *I* decided to minimize his needs by feeling he wouldn't be happy no matter what I did. That was so far from the truth - which you will see later. In every other aspect of my life, I stepped up my game – I had to *Step IT Up* in this area too. So can you.

If you are rich or poor, an atheist or a religious fanatic, and you have dated men and will continue to be involved with men, many of these dilemmas/scenarios might sound familiar to you.

After reading the last page and completing the last assignment in the book, you will have a better understanding of those types of scenarios and how it can get you, a good woman, that actually has a good man, in trouble. You can't be good at anything if you don't have the attitude and state of mind to match. That is why it is of the utmost importance to take your time in the Self Help segment and do everything that is asked of you.

Conflicted

WHAT FAMOUS PERSON HAVE I SLEPT WITH?
WHO DID I GIVE A B.J. TO AND HIS WIFE LEFT HIM?

It seems like unnecessary drama is the only way to get Information out thru main stream media. That is another reason why we are conflicted about oral sex. Society only associates the oral act with cheaters and home wreckers. Why not promote the education and the fun couples can have when we get over our oral issues and become better lovers as a result?

What I also find fascinating is that so many sistas read all the gossipy stuff about everyone's life, talk about the dysfunctions of friends, read erotic novels and wish they could be *that* character, but many of those same sistas won't read things like *this* to improve on their *own* stuff.

I'm so cool with NOT being a Video Vixen
(I just enjoy being known as the wife, '*who learned how to give Awesome Head to her Huzband*' title)

Close the book if your are the sista who's settling to be the *DIP* or the Piece on the side— This Book Won't Work for YOU!
If you're not in his heart, you can only blow one of his minds.
But, if you are in need of a comical, yet serious, education about Oral Sex, want to stop being a Selfish Lover, need more ammunition to put the DAMN THANG on your man or simply is a Good Girl that wants to learn how to love and be loved, better -
Enjoy the read. Tell a friend.
Have a Ladies Nite Out Party.

The assignments and homework in the chapters ahead have helped me and others overcome what we used to think were colossal, unclimbable mountains in our relationships. I now know that those mountains were actually specks of sand in my world. I was making my relationships more complicated than they had to be.

Chapter 1   WHY ME...

Just like me, you might be headed down the same path. This is due to our mis–education growing up into respectful young ladies. My parents, just as they were taught, told me more about what good young ladies didn't do. Unfortunately and understandably, I was never a woman in my parents' eyes, no matter what age I was. They gave great lessons to live by when I was young and single.

But what happened to this *"Speech:"*
Now that you are a grown woman, throw 98% of the things we told you about boys (not men) and sex into the recycle bin of your mind!

As a grown woman, I was perplexed in regards to if I was still on the young lady's path or the grown woman's path of life. There is a difference – I just didn't know it at the time.

That *successful* relationship talk from the married folks, the church folks or my folks, never came. Therefore, I was clueless as to showing the man that I *really* wanted… what I really *wanted* from him! By being uninformed, good girlish and secretive all my life, I was forced to put the pieces together about men, relationships and me, all by myself.

Conflicted

The Truth

No matter where women are: at work, at the park with the kids or at church; we always find a common ground to get advice on, debate over, and end great relationship with others due to justifiable and unjustifiable reasons about our children, men and sex. From the pastor's woman to the First Lady, women will come face to face with death, taxes, the dating game and giving head. Let the talk shows help you with death and taxes; I will give you the ins and outs of dating and Oral Sex. In a weird, comical sort of way, all these things are intertwined like a big ball of yarn.

Keep on being stubborn about giving head and watch yourself have major problems in the dating game. Even worse, marry a brotha who has had awesome blow jobs in the past, and it's obvious that you literally suck at giving head. Literally! That can lead to your death! Or having problems with Uncle Sam because he has gone and left you with all the bills (taxes).

And just like death and taxes...

you know if you're dating long enough that Oral Sex question is coming... **And yet, we never prepare ourselves for this, either.**

Chapter 1   WHY ME...

> The more parties I do, the more women I see; it is apparently clear we battle the Oral Sex / Good Girl dilemmas a lot more than society thinks.

Just like the majority, as a teen, I was hormoned into the dating game. And just like most young ladies (teens), when it came to sexuality and exploring my own body, I was already, at least, a decade behind the only other mammal I could legally be involved with. My parents prepared me to do well in school, but only taught me through fear about boys. I was so empty-headed, unsure and untrained in the *boy* subject.

I was being groomed to be a respectful young lady; I was taught not to boy hunt until *after* my parents thought it was appropriate for *them* to accept. We were a family on a straightened path, destined to fit into the common societal mold. Dating as a young lady was something my parents didn't want to stomach. They never wanted to see me as a sexual human being. This is the story of many sistas who search for the resolution to the Oral Sex dilemma. Indirectly, we are told by society that good girls *don't* - only bad girls *do*!

Conflicted

DO... Don't Do... What!?

All I discovered as I became a woman trying to form a successful partnership with men were all the things I thought *good girls* weren't suppose to do, were all the things good and bad men repeatedly asked me for.

This book is for all the women plagued with the
Should I or Shouldn't *I*
Oral Sex *question?*

It was written to address women like the person I used to be. If you want to tear down the walls of your sexual misconceptions to become a better partner to your man, the process can start here. Pride yourself in realizing the importance of pleasing your man in all ways possible.

> **Remember**
> Anything between the two of you is game.

Chapter 1   **WHY ME...**

This is not only a *How To* book, it is also a *Self Help* book that walks you through the process of deprogramming yourself. The person that you are now took years to develop. With a little help, it won't take long to make a change. Personal help will come from all the assignments, homework, solutions etc, that you must complete. Many of the common myths and complaints about Oral Sex will be covered in this book, along with all the pleasures and benefits that come with giving great head. You probably don't understand, at the moment, how giving head can be pleasurable or beneficial for you. Many sistas are in your shoes. I used to feel the same way, too... here's the common oral scenario:

> I am being harassed by my man to put his penis in my mouth.
> " Just suck it a *lil* bit!" he begs, standing right over me.
> All types of crazy thoughts enter my mind.
> "I can't believe this fool wants me to put his funky dick in my mouth. I don't who you've been with.
> I know this is wrong. I am not going to
> change who I am over something I've always known was nasty, long before me and this fool got together!"

We proceeded to get busy in spite of it.

> "I knew he didn't need me to suck it to get hard."
> "Hell... why *should* I! What's in it for *me*?"
> " He's going to have to prove himself to me before I even think about doing that nasty stuff!"

Conflicted

It's easy to see now, how I lost the opportunity to get to know a couple of really great guys early on. But I am thankful for those lessons and missed opportunities because it has lead me here; in a place in my life where I'm comfortable enough to write this book. Although this is a common scenario, this is the beginning of the end to a good girl's relationship - good or bad. At one of your most intimate moments with your man, instead of processing the information and thinking about what can be done to satisfy the both of you, you go back in time. You use your childhood *good girl* tales for confirmation of what *not* to do, versus conforming to the needs of you and your partner at that moment.

I've also found an inner peace and understand that the mis-education from my parents wasn't intentional, nor could I continue to blame them for the path I was on as a woman trying to maintain healthy relationships with men.

> One of your goals is redefining what a *good woman* is based on. Is a good woman based on what society thinks or what her family needs are? Definitely include your man's needs, he is a part of your family, too.

Chapter 1 **WHY ME...**

The One Emotion That Still Controls You

Think about it, while growing up, a small word that sparked an emotion from you when you were just a child, has served its purpose and now possesses power over you as an adult. This small word, this one emotion, is one of the main contributors to your Oral Sex dilemma and other things that jeopardize the success of your relationship.

What do you think it is?

_____

Conflicted

Fear keeps us from

trying

crying

even failing

and succeeding

Fear keeps us from

dying to save another

lying for a purpose

flying to new heights

Fear keeps us from saying HI

to the *one* that could have been the ONE

the one that could have helped you succeed when you were trying

gave you encouraging words when you were crying

the one who told you that failing is a natural part of life as long as you strive to keep living

FEAR... So small and yet so life changing

Written by Mz. Annjee

Now that I am much wiser, I decided to learn from other people's mistakes. I've kicked fear to the curb and created a new path for myself. My father is probably turning in his urn right now. My mother has learned to embrace the new me… we'll see if her hugs are weakened after she reads this book and realizes…

I'm a freak… JUST LIKE MY PARENTS
And I'm LOVIN IT!

Conflicted

Brief History of Oral Sex

First, the technical name for oral sex is Fellatio. Fellatio indirectly comes from the Latin word *fellare* - which means to suck. Oral sex has been in our world since the beginning of time. It has been said that we are the only mammals that perform oral sex on each other. I think we are the only mammals that realize how great it feels. I have seen some types of chimpanzees do it to each other. Who hasn't seen a dog licking each other's genitals? The differences between us and other mammals are they won't talk about or made fun of the other mammals because they suck at trying to be good lovers and satisfying their partner.

Religion has been a blessing for many people but has been a curse to our sexual health. Although various sex acts have been depicted in the Bible, in the minds of many religious followers, any act that does not result in procreation is forbidden. So oral sex is definitely out of the question. Oral Sex was associated with what society *considered* to be bad people - immoral and unchaste women or women of the night and homosexuals. And even now, although it has been around since like forever, good girls like ourselves have embedded issues *still*.

Chapter 1   **WHY ME...**

Warning... Warning...
All Dicks are Not the Same

In the beginning, when I had written only a few pages of the book, a good friend said this after reading the introduction,

"Sooo, basically, you're writing a book about Dicks!"

Maybe she picked that up from those couple of unedited pages, but some of the things I want you to take from this are:

- an understanding of why this oral thing constantly comes up in your relationships

- knowing that you can't afford to remain a selfish lover and have a *good* man

- understand your dilemmas about Oral Sex, doing what it takes to overcome them and how to become better at it and other things sexual

- in the process of finishing the book, most, if not all, of your Oral Sex issues will be addressed and you will be on your way to facing some of your mental hang–ups and trying it - AND really being good at it, too!

Conflicted

> You can still be the good girl in your parents' eyes and create the necessary evolution of becoming an awesome woman to your man.
>
> Break out of the parental handcuffs your parents subconsciously have on you. Find a new YOU and break the boring love shackles you've created in the bedroom.
>
> The greater sexual woman you were designed to be is in the making.

Chapter 1   WHY ME...

> **Let's Be Real**
> Young, old, rich or poor, everyone wants someone to at *least* try to cater to their sexual desires
> AND
> still be able to be a good mate.

Why is it so hard to give head to the man you care for?

In your teenage years, you dreamt of fame and fortune, not about who you would give head to when you became an adult. You saw yourself swaged in beautiful clothes and everything that money could buy. The hottest and sexiest body on earth was graced upon you, without a single workout or calorie count. Also in your dreams, an even richer and sexier brotha was standing by your side that *everybody* wanted - but he only had eyes for you.

We, the good girls, assumed the freaks and hoes envisioned themselves as future street walkers, home wreckers and prostitutes. Since your life was so different than the bad girl (at least you thought), you knew he wouldn't want to get involved with the hood

Conflicted

rats. Your dreams wasn't about sex… maybe just him getting to 3rd base. That satisfied your conscience as a teen because it didn't defy your parents and the going all the way thing. You still felt pure because if he didn't *hit it* (a penetrating home run) that didn't make you feel like a hoe. Finally, all your dream man needed to be satisfied was your pretty smile and an occasional 3rd base *he* attempted to make on you... when you felt like being bothered, of course.

> Stop letting movies such as Titanic and Twlight be the guidelines you use for finding love.

This type of fantasy continued into your adulthood. Today, do you still think that this scenario will help you be a better partner to your man in the real-world? What are your expectations of him and will this keep him loving you forever… forever… ever!? If you haven't realized by now, selfish dreams leads to bad relationships and yet, a lot of sistas still try to use these childhood dreams to find *Mr. Right*.

Chapter 1   **WHY ME...**

> Our dreams and reality are closely related, except we don't have to think about what that Sexy Brotha needs are. This way of thinking creates havoc in our real relationship.

Wake UP! and Smell the Burnt Microwavable Popcorn!

Performing Oral Sex on a man is a vision that we formed in our minds when most of us were scary non–sexual adolescent virgins. Just like when you were younger, you feared scary movies, but there was someone available to comfort you and explain to you how those types of movies weren't real. You eventually understood and now you can watch scary movies, knowing they're not real. Quite a few of us go out of our way to watch scary movies... although they are so predictable.

Unfortunately, no one helped us create a new vision about the big dirty man wanting us to suck his hairy lil thing because it has never stopped being *'taboo'*. Instead of people trying to explain relationships to you, you still live in fear. We base our adult relationships on our young nasty thoughts about sex and boys. This repetitive

Conflicted

scenario is similar to that scary movie, the outcome of you not giving him head is always the same - he wants it more and you both are frustrated over the Oral Sex thing.

In your mind, it's still hard to tell truth from fiction. Most of the stories you were told, you found out to be untrue due to your now firsthand experience. When it came to the nastiness of boys, puberty kicked in and it was hard as hell to stop being a human with hormones and needs. Although good women have many sexual and relationship setbacks, you learned by having sex that sex wasn't as bad as your parents made it seem. You had to face it, if done correctly, physically sex felt good. Now mentally, it's a whole other story. From there, you were able to draw your own opinion and generate better visions of love, men, sex and relationships in your mind.

> You were provided comfort about scary movies...
> and now you are uncertain about this *blow job* thing.
> Once again, give it a try, learn by experience...
> it's not as bad as you think!

Chapter 1   **WHY ME...**

What about the blow job?

The thought of giving head became more disgusting as you went through puberty and you naturally started to like boys. No one told you any different about the nasty Oral Sex craze that was the talk around the school. The only ones that you heard that gave head were freaks, hoes, bus downs, hood rats and sluts. Of course, that was an obvious solvable situation - you wouldn't ever do that! You're not a *bus–down*!

The *No Blow Job* conformation also came from the silly lil nasty boys in high school. They were the ones that said you were a hoe if you did it. Those same silly boys are now men wishing they never said those words. Many of these men married good girls with the unrealistic expectations that they would morph into a freak at their command with the ability to fulfill their every fantasy. Fathers, brothers and husbands never knew the difference between the women they called hoes versus the good girl that could have been taught to have an open mind with one man. They are regretting it now because they know an awesome blow job can come from the woman they love, the mother of their children, versus a hoe or

Conflicted

mistress they have no ties with. You can place some of the blame on men for your present situation. This continued old fashioned thinking, is one of the reasons why I, the *ex* good girl turned better partner, wrote *this* book about oral sex first. And this crazy misconception that many brothas are still taught to believe in—I'm convinced, is one of the reasons why some men cheat and feel that it's justifiable.

In your mind, the boys spreading rumors about the girls who did was your proof that blow jobs weren't for you. Remember, the same girls that gave blow jobs in H.S, also put out. You never heard about them being bad at it, either. Nor did the fellas stop going to her. We still carry out our young H.S patterns.

After you realized how good sex could feel, you didn't compare the sex act with bad girls anymore. And if you did compare yourself to the bad girl because you were having sex, you probably made it your mission not to enjoy sex/lovemaking as much as you could have. No matter how positive our experience can be with our man, we still can't get over the grammar/high school *blow job* dilemma.

Chapter 1   **WHY ME...**

The Bottom Line Is

3rd base and over–moistened panties is now a joke and you know what *Horny* truly feels like when you don't get any!

NOW

You realize you have needs and a man that can score a home run to your satisfaction is essential to you. The man in your dreams is now the man by your side and he has the same needs as you and he too wants satisfaction.

ALSO KNOW

You, other Good Girls, the Bad Girl and the Mistress have the same bills, want the same things and want the same man.

REALIZE

It's nothing wrong with a good girl that will give her man what he wants AND needs.

YOU MUST REALIZE TO STAY AHEAD

Knowing how to blow *Both* of your man's minds is a must

Conflicted

Now, how does a blow job benefit *you*?

In a sense, it really doesn't! There are no nerve endings around your mouth that produces pleasure for you when doing it. You cannot gauge his pleasures by *your* own. And if you don't do it often, your jaws will probably hurt. And, when a brotha cumes... that's one of the ugliest faces you'll *love* to see him make. The ugliest, yet most sexiest face your man will make for you because you made it happen. Pleasing him, like he tries to please you sexually, is what's in it for you. Being turned on and excited because you have matured beyond the teenage phase and stepped into a world of two sexual adults not being influenced by what mommy and daddy told you... PRICELESS! The willingness to satisfy each other in that way, opens up the lines of communication to a whole other level. That's what's in it for you! If that is not enough... accept that
"You Are A Selfish Lover!" You might proudly boost that you are selfish, but is that working for your relationship? I DOUBT IT!

STOP the 8 Track Mentality - You MUST CHANGE!

Chapter 1   **WHY ME...**

The Unavoidable Question with Fixable Solutions

When that certain Oral Sex question is asked at my Hen Parties, some women listen quietly, looking for answers. Others voice their opinions and concerns. Unfortunately, there are also a few ladies that leave the room at this point and start to eat and drink. I'm still not sure if they're just not interested in change or if they feel their man doesn't care about how good they are in this area.

> No matter what happens in your relationship, always listen to free advice and the thoughts of others. When you do, you will realize you are not alone when it comes to many concerns in your relationship. Most things are truly fixable.
> It's always easier to hear others voicing their concerns and opinions, but what about yours?

Answer the Question

> "Why don't you like to perform Oral Sex on your man as much as he would like you to?"

Fixable Dilemmas and Solutions

STOP
DON'T GO ANY FURTHER

You must take time out and write down your reasons. In order to help yourself, you must acknowledge your dilemma. After you write your reasons down, look at the following page to see if it has been addressed.
YOUR GOAL is to try to overcome your fears. Do the homework/assignments for your reason, then read the entire chapter and do all the homework/assignments.

This will only take a couple of seconds to complete
U Can Do It!

Chapter 2   **I Can't Because...**

REASONS

Why don't YOU
(not what you've heard)
like to perform Oral Sex on your man as much as he would like you to?

1. _____

2. _____

3. _____

4. _____

5. _____

If at least two of your concerns have not been covered
In this segment, please email them to me:
(vsgseries@yahoo.com)

Fixable Dilemmas and Solutions

> **IF** your reason(s) are not listed, go to www.VSGseries.com and email your reason(s). I will research and find an answer to your dilemma(s).
> Also, go to the site and feel free to give advice, tips and techniques.
> We will blog together.
> Look for various polls, forums and resources to help you and your sweetie.

When you need the 411 on relationships, taboo topics and how sistas and brothas think - I'm your Gal

Chapter 2   **I Can't Because...**

Bring Out Your ORAL Diva
Should I OR Shouldn't I

Here's *The List* of the most common reasons heard over the years as to why women have issues about Oral Sex, along with *Fixable Solutions* for you

- My jaws and hands hurt
- I just don't have the time... Because of the Kids
- I'm tired after work
- I am... I just can't do that *right now*
- He wants it too much! It takes too long
- I will do it when I want to
- He doesn't deserve it
- I am a victim of sexual abuse
- I don't know what I'm doing
- His balls and dick smell musty, I will get sick
- His penis doesn't look right... He's not circumcised!
- I don't want to kiss my kids if I do something like that
- I don't want him to cume in my mouth

Read ALL Reasons for knowledge

Fixable Dilemmas and Solutions

1ST ASSIGNMENT

In order for you to *even attempt* to make a change in your oral dilemma

YOU MUST

look at the male anatomy in a different light

YOU MUST

touch, admire and explore your
man's mind & body
and think positive about what you do to him

and YOU MUST STOP

feeling bad about it

Assignment/Homework

My jaws and hands hurt

Fixable! You tend to have aches and pains when you do something every once in a while, versus often. You have to ask yourself, how often do you really give your man a blow job? If you can't remember; it's been too long. Spank yourself and say
"*Bad Girlfriend*!" If you do it only twice a year, once on his birthday and on the fourth of July because you were wasted...
Bad Girlfriend! If this sounds like you, be prepared to come face-to-face with lock jaw.

<u>Solution:</u> <u>Practice!</u> <u>Practice!</u> Practice!

That could be the remedy to stop the aches and pain. First, stretch your Oris Orbicularis and Buccinator (your mouth muscles) by opening as wide as you can and closing your mouth repeatedly. If you don't want to look so obvious in public when you are practicing your blow job exercises; then open your mouth wider for a juicy sour Granny Smith apple or stretch your mouth over a large polish or a popsicle. Cold, sweet and juicy things can work wonders for

Fixable Dilemmas and Solutions

sore cheeks. If you really want to keep your jaws fit, munch on some trail mix that consists of various types of nuts, oatmeal and raisins. That will not only keep you healthy, but your jaws will be ready for action at any moment.

Lubricants work wonders for tired jaws, also. It helps your mouth slide right over that hard juicy polish (his penis). Water based lubes are good, but silicone based lubes are superb and can help him cume a lot faster than without. And if you are in need of a little help with the taste… flavored lubricants could be perfect for you. I go into detail about things like this in the chapter 6 ***The Sticky Ickey.***

> Now, if months have passed and your mouth is constantly full of fruits, nuts, vegetables and oats as you chew to the theme song from the movie *Rocky*, but still you give no sucky sucky…
> that really wasn't it…
> *Face It! You're Still Scured!!*

Have a Hen or Couples Party
Find a Rep in your area
Or just need Love advice
www.VSGseries.com

Chapter 2   I Can't Because...

Homework

It's time to open up to your man

By now you know this is an issue that you are trying to resolve in your relationship, so this conversation is long overdue.

It's time for *The Talk*. Start off by simply saying...

You're working on being a better partner to him. Tell him you are currently reading a book about Oral Sex and there will be times you need his support and patience. He will have to be willing to show and tell you how to satisfy him orally. Also say, you are learning how to step out of your box and get a lil wild. Say, "I want you to join me; don't make me feel bad by teasing me." Stress to him providing knowledge of what turns him on is essential in helping you overcome your issues with Oral Sex. You also want to be able to talk about some of the things that turn you on and incorporate it into the Oral Sex and foreplay sessions.

Tell him the book consists of a series of assignments that you must complete. Some assignments might require his participation, while others might require him to become your teacher.

Find out what he calls it (them)... his penis and his two buddies. Every penis and balls have a name. If you want, make up your own name. Make sure your name(s) doesn't offend him and discourage you from doing what you need to orally. Always use MR... if in front of the kids (when talking about his body parts) so it's your lil secret love code.

Tell us the results of your *talk*
www.VSGseries.com

Assignment/Homework

Assignment

You must get comfortable looking at the male anatomy

A major battle women have is not looking at a man nude or their man's body as being something beautiful, natural and normal. Yeah, some women will say they look at men all the time... that's true to some extent. Who hasn't seen a rock hard chest, chiseled stomach or a handsome face on a brotha? But what do you think of when you see an un erect or erect penis? How do you respond if he's standing in front of you, bucket naked, with his penis directly in your face? What do you feel when you see the inside of your man's butt (ass - for the ones who call it that)? How do you feel when you see your man's anus (the hole)? Most of us feel uncomfortable and even nauseous when looking at the bottom half of a man's (waist down to the toes). Many women become uncomfortable after a little boy learns how to wipe himself. It's the same parts... just a lot bigger with hair, *hopefully*?!

> We don't want to lick or suck anything below his waist. You must get comfortable with his anatomy as a whole, in order to be comfortable with oral sex.

Assignment/Homework

I just don't have the time... Because of the Kids

Fixable! Do it *before* work! Do it *before* you take the kids out! Have your man help out with the kids and do it afterwards. Instead of always taking the kids out in a public setting, let them play in the house or in the back yard. If you don't want them in the back yard... you set it off with your sweetie behind the bushes while the kids are in the house. You work like crazy to pay the mortgage...

Damn It! Live in the house and go *Wild* sometimes!

Make your man *feel* like he's 1st priority to you - especially when you always say "*you don't have the time!*" Making him *feel* like he's top on your *To Do* list is achieved by the quality time you spend with him and not constantly reiterating that God, the kids, and the bills, are your first priorities. **Your man is not elated knowing he's not even in your top two.** We constantly find time for the things we really want to do, so we can find time for the things our man likes, too.

Fixable Dilemmas and Solutions

Although this is a book about Oral Sex... there's a bigger picture, make your man a priority and give a brotha a blow job and all the other things that come with keeping the relationship strong.

Assignment

Make him feel he's your top priority

List 2 things you can do to make him feel like he is your Top Priority

> example: making him a plate while you both watch a program he likes

1. _____
2. _____

List 2 things that you can say that he will know you appreciate him

> example: when you are feeling pressured, he keeps the kids out your hair for a while

1. _____
2. _____

Assignment/Homework

Homework

Make him feel he's your top priority

The very next time you see your man, give him a hug and a kiss on the lips and say "Baby! I appreciate you sooo much!" Be able to say at least two things to confirm your statement and do at least one of the things you listed in the previous assignment that you know will make him feel like he is your top priority.

Purpose:
Men tend to be more understanding when they feel that you are sincere and actually appreciate what they do and admire who they are.

Document his behavior:
Did it work? Could you do things differently to produce the results you want?

_____
_____
_____
_____
_____

Relationship Goal:
Incorporate this into the New You

Have any questions - email me

Assignment/Homework

Observe and Write

Whatever you write down is to make your relationship better. Be willing to compromise.

Save the original... MAKE COPIES

Assignment/Homework

> **You must embrace finding time for his satisfaction. If you don't, he will eventually start to resent you.**

I'm tired after work

There's not enough time in the day for sistas to get everything done. When you must be a part of:

- ✓ 12 hr work days - this consists of preparing for and getting to and from work
- ✓ 6 hrs of sleep, if you're lucky
- ✓ 6 hrs left to try to be super mom, doctor, manager, referee, cook, and the family planner for the days ahead

not to mention the roller-coaster of emotions and stress of the day. It's really understandable when women complain about the *time thing*. BUT! No matter how much we complain, we still get the things done, especially the ones we feel are important.

If you are like many sistas, myself included, you probably complain about being tired all day long, so being freaky or being his best friend isn't always on your *To Do List*. When you have housework, homework and work from home, everyone in the house should be glad you just don't one day up and leave forever.

Fixable Dilemmas and Solutions

Also, another thing that should concern you is we (ladies) don't pat ourselves on the back enough and say "I did an awesome job and it's time for some *ME* time!" Nor do we acknowledge when we are actually placing our man dead last on our *To Do List* and we should be saying "it's cuddle time for me and *my baby*!"

> **Solution:**
> Make Oral Sex a treat for the both of you. Do the Alternative 69 position or the Everything and More Pretzel #2 position, have him use a toy on you for clitoral orgasmic stimulation as he fondles all your other erogenous zones. Make time for you both to cume and you will have the best sleep ever!
>
> **Note:** These Awesome positions and more can be found in Chapter 7

No matter how tired women are, we still muster up the energy from somewhere and achieve many things. You are tired of attending all your children's school functions, church and family functions and other functions that you really don't want to be a part of, but you do! And yet, with all that extra stuff, women still muster up the energy to work a 9-5. That paycheck, bad or good, is the motivating factor that makes us push through the tiredness.

Being our children's biggest fan and helping in the creation of making them better adults is invaluable. Our inspiration to overcome our tiredness is knowing that we will be proud of them one day and they will successfully leave the parental nest... *we hope*.

Our extended families – the church and people outside our immediate family are also in need of our help. We cook, decorate, sing usher, etc for our faith and no matter how tired we are, we worship our faith on a regular basis. The pay off in overcoming our tiredness with this is that it makes us feel good and we are closer to our faith and the people around us. At that moment, the people around us make us feel special and appreciated.

In order to solve this fixable *"I'm to tired to give a blow job"* problem, you have to realize if your tiredness is a reason that constantly pops up when it's time to satisfy him, it's simply an excuse.

> **Misconception:**
> A good woman is someone who takes care of the kids and keeps the house clean. The bestiest woman doesn't forget to be the freak in the bedroom and her man's best friend. Unfortunately, many good women don't learn about the freak thing until a couple of failed relationships and bitter divorces later.

Why when the time comes to tap into our energy source in every other situation, it's second nature, but when it comes to our man, we take our relationship for granted? When it's time to do a lil *sucky*

Fixable Dilemmas and Solutions

sucky, we *ducky ducky.* Why is it so hard to overcome the tiredness for your man? It's simple! No one ever discussed the importance of your man and the *"I'm gonna tell the world"* praises that are just as important for him to hear YOU proudly say. Mis informed sistas would say "I'm not about to do anything extra for *that man,* he can leave at any time."

When it comes to *that man,* bad or good, many ladies are in relationships with *that man.* Not putting him first, in the same way you expect from him, says a lot. Remember, *that man* can say the same about you to justify what he won't do. A lot of sistas feel that they do cater to their man and they give him more time than their children. Sistas feel this way because they routinely fix his favorite meals. Women spend sometimes up to $200.00 for this feast, hours shopping and preparing for this one mouth-watering meal that only you can do - so you've been made have to believe. After you finish slaving in the kitchen, you fix his plate and you both dine for about a half an hour. Damn! After that, comes the cleaning, putting up the food and he still wants you to break him off with a lil sucky, sucky and some sex.

You are exhausted and in your mind, he doesn't appreciate you because he still wants more (the sucky, sucky and sex). We've been taught that pleasing your man is making his favorite foods and keeping his stomach full. And that has some truth to it. But we don't ask him what he wants, with specific options given because we don't really want to hear the truth.

Women enjoy bragging rights, too. It feels good when you can boost to other ladies and men about how you cook (the good girl version of catering to) for your man. And it makes you feel good when he makes some of the fellas envious by taking a plate to work and boasting about what you cooked for him.

But how much time did you *actually* spend catering to him? How much time was *actually* spent on intimate conversations? Not much, when you really think about it. What made you tired? It was the preparations, slaving and the clean up! It wasn't anything relating to the *actual* mental or physical satisfaction of your man.

Cooking is fine, but if you'd ask your man what he'd prefer– and you didn't get mad over his choice– he'd tell you he wanted a small meal AND an awesome blow job AND great sex AND he wants to see you enjoying doing them ALL. *Men don't want to choose.* Trust me, but if he had to choose, a man will miss a meal for an awesome blow job any day. Just watch episodes of *Cheaters*. Why does your man have to choose, anyway? Tradition has its place sometimes, but cook less and love each other more. I guarantee, it will keep you both healthier, happier and not so tired.

Fixable Dilemmas and Solutions

Solution
Think Out the Box
Work Smarter, NOT Harder

All the time, energy and money it takes to fix his favorite meal can now go to his favorite restaurant–the ones that have the specials where two can eat for $30 or less. Have intimate conversations on the ride to the restaurant, as you wait for your food, while you're eating and on the ride home. Make sure you bring a doggy bag home. Watch your favorite shows together for as long as you like. Do you notice, you haven't lifted a finger in work, so you're not tired. Take a couple of minutes to give your man an awesome blow job. Now, there's enough time for you to get yours. You can fall asleep in each other's arms.

All this is done in half the time, energy and price than the *old* good girl way.

The Benefit: This new way is twice the fun, twice the caloric burn, twice the orgasms with more time to sleep.

New bragging rights: You thought out of your box and he ate his favorite foods *twice*, you had the energy for intimate conversations and your were each other's dessert. You slept peacefully in each other's arm. Send him to work with his doggy bag and every bite he takes, he will think about you and that night over and over again anticipating the next time.

The woman that is truly envied is the woman that is confident enough not to be ashamed of loving her man and showing him a good time and not being concerned about what others think.

Now, if you still can't muster up the energy to give your man oral... **FACE IT, You Just Don't Want To**

Chapter 2   I Can't Because...

Bring Out Your ORAL Diva
Should I OR Shouldn't I

> When it comes to Oral Sex,
> no one encourages you to do it and you are embarrassed to brag about it.
> Nor do you want him to talk about it...
> I guarantee he will appreciate you more, when you do.
> Let a restaurant feed him sometimes and *you* give the awesome blows jobs, versus the opposite.

Since you can overcome the tiredness in all other areas with a smile on your face, you must do the same here, too.

Another reason I've heard is

"I am... I just can't do that *right now*!"

Same as the *tired* excuse, it just sounds better. Is it ok to *always* expect him to *understand* why you should be given a pass in regards to his pleasure? *Right Now*, for him, never comes soon enough. But inserting himself inside you you think is pleasurable for the both of you; that is one of the reasons why intercourse is the first choice for many women. Give him first choice sometimes. No matter what else you do, Oral Sex is foreplay for a man. It only takes a couple of hand stroking and mouth sucking moments to quickly satisfy him.

Fixable Dilemmas and Solutions

> ***Suck it up***
> muster up the time and energy
> like you always do
> for everyone else...
> your relationship depends on it.

A good relationship with your man is the one investment you don't realize its value until it's gone. A man who feels like you don't have time for him; will have a negative impact on your life.

There is a high percentage of couples who separate over sexual and emotional neglect. I like to call it
Irreconcilable Differences.

Bring Out Your ORAL Diva
Should I OR Shouldn't I

Your Payment

in making this happen is a good relationship, a closer bond between the two of you and the confidence in knowing how to satisfy your man. A woman and a man working together as a family usually does better financially, emotionally and their children benefit beyond measures...

NOW That's Priceless

Fixable Dilemmas and Solutions

He wants it too much! It takes too long!

How much time do you *actually* invest in your relationship on a daily basis? This should not include: cooking meals, paying bills, doing chores or taking care of the kids. What is the *actual* time YOU initiate intimate moments between the two of you, from:

- *asking* how his day went
- *really listening* to what he has to say
- *being interested* in the things that interest him

How often do YOU *really* come into his world? If you're thinking *"What About Me,"* it's not about you right now. When you complete the time sheet, don't think angrily about what he is *not* doing for you and make excuses as to why you don't do things for him. Just keep in mind, behind every good man, is a better woman—YOU!

> If you wrote down *time* being one of your dilemmas, your goal is to analyze your schedule and make room for you, your man and pleasures you both deserve.

Before you create a time sheet for you and your man, write down what you feel usually happens on an average day. Your goal is to actually observe how your man really is for an entire week. You and your man are more predictable than you think.

Chapter 2   I Can't Because...

You want to find out when he is more likely to ask you for Oral Sex and what you are doing at the moment he asks. Within the next 24 hours, write down on the time sheet what has actually happened this day. Let the day flow naturally. Write down what he does, how your day flows in regards to you, your children and him. Do not force an intimate moment between the two of you. This will tell you how much time you actually spend with each other and if the saying is really true, *he wants it too much*! If he doesn't know you're in the room, then that means your lives have been separated by everything else... *that's not good!*

You might realize he doesn't ask for oral several times a day like you thought. You might also observe that he doesn't ask you when you are in mid run of doing something like you continuously complain about. It could become apparently clear that he asks when everything has calmed down and you still say "he wants it too much!" If it takes to long, you must improve on your technique and attitude. You will work on those areas later in the book.

> Create ways you can incorporate more quality time together that will also include…
> **YEP! A lil' sucky sucky
> from the both of you.**

Fixable Dilemmas and Solutions

Change Starts with YOU... Right NOW!

Observe and Write

Save the original... MAKE COPIES

Whatever you write down is to make your relationship Better. Be willing to compromise.

Assignment/Homework

Bring Out Your ORAL Diva
Should I OR Shouldn't I

> **Note:**
>
> Make Oral Sex a part of your weekly (YES! Weekly)
> schedule and he won't ask you for it as much.
>
> **
>
> If You are initiating Oral Sex, you are in control of being satisfied, too.
>
> **
>
> Sometimes when you don't make it *all about you...*
> You can receive even more pleasure.

Fixable Dilemmas and Solutions

Assignment

Before you create a time sheet for you and your man, write down what you feel usually happens on an average day. As I stated earlier, your goal is to actually observe how your man is for an entire week. Again, the both of you are more predictable than you think. Critique your time, tell him what you can do to add time for him and the both of you give suggestions how to make time for each other. This schedule is relating to *Time Dilemma*.

You can also
download additional things online

Homework

YOUR Man YOUR Time YOUR Schedule

Create Your New Schedule

Create more quality time with your man. Make a schedule emphasizing you and your man only. Commit to at least two days out the week where you can give quality time to one another. Do things that are not kid friendly. Yep! for starters, 1 blow job once a week for no reason (Twice that week, if it's his birthday). If you want it to lead to something else after you finish… tell him it's your turn to receive!

receive and share ideas at
www.VSGseries.com

Assignment/Homework

Appreciate the fact

that your man has come to you and asked you, his woman, to please him. No one should have to feel like a child in an adult relationship. Your man should not have to beg or explain the reasons why he should receive a blow job, and you should not make him feel guilty when he wants it more than you want to give it.

Fixable Dilemmas and Solutions

www.VSGseries.com
Change Starts with YOU... Right NOW!

Save the original... MAKE COPIES	weekly motivational relationship message		
	Wk: _____		

Assignment/Homework

Small Steps equals Big Success
NOT Forbidden

Month:

Assignment/Homework

Interesting Party Info:

I have found that many couples spend less than 1/2 hour a day actually talking about their interests to each other. Many couples do not discuss how their day went and even less time is spent on just holding hands or hugging one another. Cuddling up to watch a favorite show or laughing together is obsolete now. For the most part, couples don't do things as a couple; they are together only as parents, raising children. Realistically, we spend more time traveling with strangers, as we go to and from work.

The most intimate moments are now being shared with co-workers because co workers (females *and* males) eagerly listen to one another to avoid thinking about the stresses of the job and family. It only takes one conversation from a sista to peak a brotha's interest.

There is not a place that I know of where sex and relationships, bad or good, is not a common conversation amongst the opposite sex/co-workers. This is the reason why the workplace is the #1 place where affairs start.

Chapter 2   I Can't Because...

Answer the following: *Do you know more single women or married women? Do you know more unhappy couples or happy couples?* If you know more married couples living happily ever after... you are definitely in the minority. And if this is true, a good sex life must be in the *happily ever after* equation.

Parents individually spend more time talking to, preparing for and thinking about their children, versus doing parenting as a team. Quality time is *not* invested in chores, bills, and planning out what we're going to wear. Before we consciously put forth the effort to give less than ½ hour of quality time a day to come into our partner's (each other's) world; we have devoted 23 1/2 hrs of our day indulged in many things that won't make a difference in the quality of the relationship. Over time, if you lose focus of the bigger picture, you can see what 23 ½ hrs a day at least 5 days a week of separation, for years, can do on a relationship that had great potential for forever after.

Fixable Dilemmas and Solutions

Bring Out Your ORAL Diva
Should I OR Shouldn't I

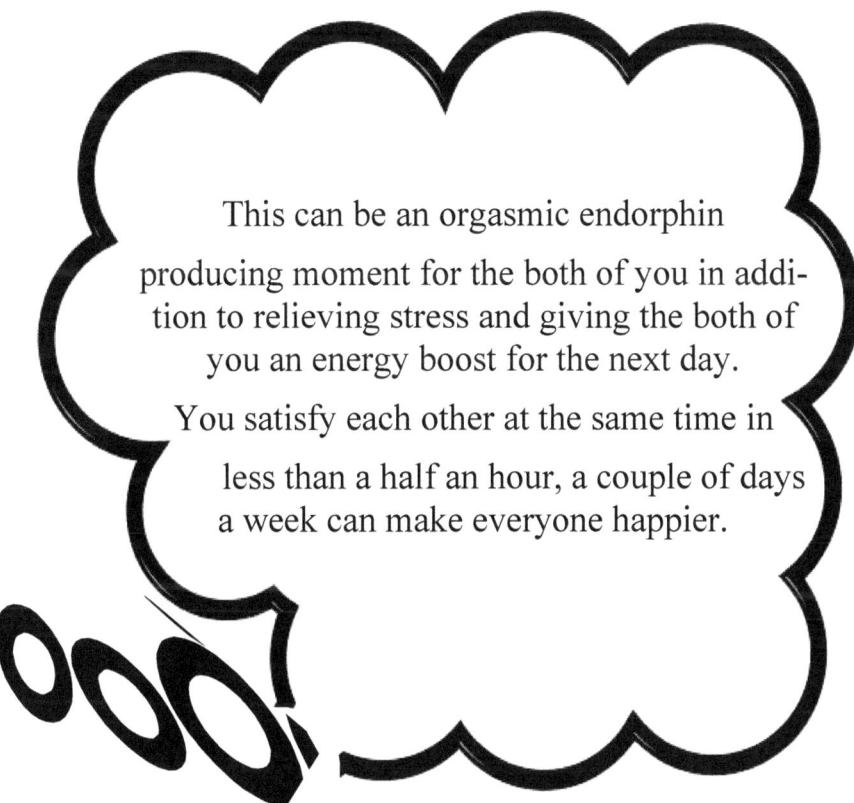

This can be an orgasmic endorphin producing moment for the both of you in addition to relieving stress and giving the both of you an energy boost for the next day. You satisfy each other at the same time in less than a half an hour, a couple of days a week can make everyone happier.

All you need is 15-30 minutes, a couple of times a week (daily if you prefer), to eliminate some of your daily stress.

Fixable Dilemmas and Solutions

I will do it when I want to:

You come off as controlling, childish and selfish.

Fixable! Come on sista… this is not the time nor place to be selfish. You have to accept that you are in a relationship, a partnership with your man. Sometimes it is not about you or what you want and when you want to do it. That also counts for him also, but at the moment, this is about you solving your oral dilemma. No one is forced to do the things they love. Learn how to love giving oral sex; no different than you love your relationship.

A rule to live by - Give What You Expect

How would you feel if the times you wanted to cuddle, make love or as you were just expecting him to go down on you… at that moment, he angrily said, "Damn! Stop Asking Me! I'll Do It When I Feel Like it!" That relationship wouldn't sit well with you… and it shouldn't be ok for him, either.

NOT Forbidden

Assignment

1. What special Holidays/Occasions is he allowed to ask you for a blow job... without you trippin?

   _____

2. How does he know when you are ready to give him oral, since you don't want him to ask for it?

   _____

   _____

3. How often do you pull his pants down, whip it out and start playing with it and sucking on that beautiful piece of artwork (your man's penis)?

   _____

4. Is the number of blow jobs comparable with what he wants to get from you?

   _____

Assignment/Homework

Interesting info

Men between the ages of 18 to 59 think about sex daily while about 25% of women think about sex on a daily basis. Unfortunately, there is no poll that shows how often men think about oral sex only, but I'm convinced the less he gets it, the more he craves it and the unhappier he gets when you say *"I will do it when I feel like it!"*

Misconceptions: When I ask women how often does their man want oral, most women say *"he wants it every day."* Although some men would surely be delighted receiving Oral Sex on a daily basis, most men would accept it being a lot less than daily, but definitely needs it more than once a month.

Solution: Communicate more and compromise. Don't be afraid to ask him about how much more (realistically) he wants Oral Sex from you. If you are nowhere near those numbers; increase the amount of times you initiate it and don't be offended if he asks for it a little more often after that. This is your perfect opportunity to negotiate things you also want from him sexually. This is the time to add some love excitement. Step out the bedroom into new heights.

Statistical resources: WebMD

He doesn't deserve it

Fixable! You are battling control, trust and anger issues.

No one *deserves* a blow job… either you *will* or you *won't*. When we hold back our feelings sexually, it usually means that we are afraid to be vulnerable. As long as we have that dangling carrot that he jumps for, we feel we are in control of him. Your man can never jump through enough hoops to make you feel good about something (Oral Sex) you were taught was wrong long before you met him. If you haven't learned by now, a man will eventually stop jumping for that dangling carrot (the promise to give him a blow job). Either you will be forced to face your fears and give head or you will do what so many women have done before you – *sabotage yet another good relationship over somethin so simple*.

Sabotage Prevails

Now you can't stop wondering why he doesn't ask you for a blow job anymore. Instead of realizing by now he knows how you will respond if he asks for Oral Sex. You switch it around, at that

Fixable Dilemmas and Solutions

moment, you feel he's cheating on you because he's not begging you for oral anymore. Your mistrust soon justifies your anger that all men are alike… DOGS! And, that becomes one of your rationales as to why you don't give head. What you said you wanted initially, you got – your man not asking you for head. And still you have an issue because he stopped asking!

It doesn't make sense! So many great women lose great men because they sabotage their own relationship without realizing their never changing patterns.

Assignment He Doesn't Deserve It

List 1-3 reasons why he doesn't deserve Oral Sex from you.

1. _____

2. _____

3. _____

This truth can set you free

Assignment/Homework

Ask Yourself

Honestly, will any of the reasons *why you don't* change or stop if you keep saying *no* to him?

OR

Are the reasons you gave preexisting; meaning they were there before you became serious and have not changed as the relationship continued, nor have you left because of it? Are these old predictable patterns *before* you got involved with him?

OR

Are these new reasons that were unpredictable or unforeseen *after* you became serious? Will saying "he does not deserve it" help your relationship with him? Will saying that resolve the issue/reasons? Can the issues be resolved in a timely matter? If not, what is the final scenario, in regards to your relationship with him? If you separate, what will you do when the next brotha ask you for the same things?

> **In some cases, the reasons that women listed are not new but have been there since the beginning of the relationship. By holding out, nothing will ever get better between the two of you. I am sure your man is worth keeping since you are reading this book. You must voice your concerns and let him voice his, peacefully, with the sole intent to resolve the issues and go on with your relationship.**

Assignment/Homework

I am a victim of sexual abuse...

I sympathize with the ordeal you went through. You must seek professional help if this is affecting your life and relationship; your livelihood depends on it. Some things you cannot—should not handle on your own. And, although prayer can help with some things sometimes, it does not replace professional counseling and talking to and with people that will give you the mental and emotional tools you need to get your power back. Sexual abuse is a life changing situation. Many women who have been victimized tend to suffer from a variety of other sexual dysfunctions. Sometimes your mind will not let you escape those moments in time. And without proper counseling, it's hard to differentiate between the intimate acts of your lover versus the sexual abuse of the attacker.

I urge you once again, seek the help of a professional therapist that specializes in the specific ordeal you've gone through. No matter what a person goes through, the weight of the incident impacts everyone. That includes your partner. Even the most understanding man still has mental, emotional and sexual needs. Before your ordeal, you probably considered your life to be very normal, meaning you also had needs that you wanted to be met by your partner, as well. If he didn't try to met your needs, that changed how you felt about the relationship.

The healing process can take time, but at the same time, it can also become a blurred line between healing and fear of gaining your power back. You must seek professional help if you want your relationship to survive. Also, have him attend some of the counseling sessions to get a better understanding of how to help you and the relationship. Any type of abuse is a hard subject to deal with - you don't necessarily have to forget, but you must learn how to go on with your life; your future is at stake. I am aware of how many times I've spoken about seeking professional help; but, I know it can take a person several times to see, read or hear something before one take action. Have I said it enough yet!? Take ACTION!

This is where it is going to seem like I am non-caring... trust me, I do care. But, what I've noticed over the years is that I hear many women *claim* to have been abused. I say *claimed* because these women have told me at parties that they just say that so they are not pressured into giving Oral Sex. And some have actually been abused as a child, but that is not the reason why they don't want to perform Oral Sex. They just think doing oral to *him* is nasty, not pleasurable for the woman and it just isn't necessary.

Can you believe it! It's true! Where women go wrong and cause a problem in their relationship is when they have their legs open and ready to receive oral, but mention the memories of rape or abuse when it's their turn to return the favor. I am disappointed with those

Fixable Dilemmas and Solutions

women. They use emotional incidents to pull on the sympathy strings of a man who is probably into her and just wants the same pleasure he repeatedly has given. This is extremely selfish! You do have options. Overcome your fears and discuss your *real* concerns about what he's asking from you OR look for a brotha that truly doesn't mind giving and giving and giving and never receiving without your fear of him cheating. If you have a brotha like that and he doesn't complain about your selfish ways; grab onto him and hold him with all your might... never let him go. There's only a handful under the age of 75 left in the *entire* world.

Now, if you are having a problem overcoming the fear of being involved with a person in a sexual manner, due to your past, again I say to seek the help of a professional therapist. If the act of giving Oral Sex is a major issue when it comes to your man, I recommend that you read this book, complete all the activities and talk honestly with your man. I get women together and talk about these types of issues constantly, so understand, you are not alone in this.

Don't make the mistake that many sistas do; you don't want him to perform Oral Sex on you in fear that he might ask for the favor in return. In many cases, a man that enjoys receiving oral also enjoys giving oral. If you choose not to start with self-help, just remember, your situation will not get any better because just like you, he has emotional, mental, and physical needs, as well.

Chapter 2 **I Can't Because...**

Is it an acceptable requirement for your mate to go down on you, but you won't seek help for your oral hang ups? You have to be honest with yourself - if this book and/or talking to him does not help you gradually overcome your dilemma, you should seek help from a therapist OR make it your mission not to get involved with men that enjoy Oral Sex. There are a couple of brothas out there that don't enjoy receiving oral. Just remember, everything has a trade-off. I don't know what the trade-off is for a brotha who doesn't want to receive a blow job; he probably doesn't want to give Oral Sex either. And he probably will have many other hang–ups, like outdated dating rituals that won't improve your relation ship...

But Hey! At least, NO BLOW JOBS for YOU!!

For the ladies who are suffering from their selfish ways - and you know who you are - STOP LYING TO MEN! The man you lied to might get involved with a woman that really has been sexually victimized and due to the mixed message he had with you, this could affect the outcome of his new relationship.

> **Many sistas could care less about what happens to a brotha *after* they are finished with him.**
> **Just remember,**
> ***karma* ain't nothing nice.**

Fixable Dilemmas and Solutions

I do not know what I'm doing

That is to be expected. Giving great head and being awesome in the bedroom is not like the Matrix; you can't plug a disk into your brain and expect to be the 'Oral Diva of the Universe'. Being good at anything takes practice. Most importantly, you have to be willing to listen to what your partner is telling you that he wants.

Break Down of the Blow Job Woes.

40% **of the BJ Woes** is the negative attitude you project *before* you even go down on him and the mental hang-ups you must overcome about oral sex being wrong.

> **Oral Sex is just another form of foreplay/lovemaking with that special someone.**

30% **of the BJ Woes** is being able to listen, without being intimidated; follow directions and tune into how his body responds to certain things you do.

> **This is not the time for jealous thoughts. It doesn't matter what he is thinking about. This is the time to monitor his responses and work on your oral craft.**

Chapter 2   I Can't Because...

Bring Out Your ORAL Diva
Should I OR Shouldn't I

15% of the BJ Woes is you making him feel like you actually enjoy giving him oral versus making him feel like his dick just came out of a trashcan filled with toxic waste. What you think about his penis and the oral sex act itself, will affect your movements and your mood. The way you look at his penis before ever giving head will affect your actions and alter his mood. Understand that your reactions speaks louder than words.

When you interrupt the blow job every two seconds to pull out every single strand of his pubic hair from your mouth with disgust on your face - this makes him feel like *maybe* you really don't want to do it. One of his biggest ballbuster moments is when you prepare to give him one of those awesome yearly blow jobs, you overstuff your mouth with mints and lozenges so you can take in as little of his penis as possible. And to top it off, you have nicely prepared a bed full of tissues, napkins and bath towels to be ready to vomit on, at a seconds notice, if any foreign fluids enters your mouth.

OR

You do another one of his ballbusting favorites - a running dash to spit out his fluids into the toilet like a sailor.

After all that, even the most secure and confident man will feel self conscious and unwanted.

Fixable Dilemmas and Solutions

> If your goal is to make him feel self conscious, offended and completely turned off... GOOD JOB!! Keep doing that and "You'll be single in NO Time!" If your goal is to be a good lover to your man, then, redo the homework/assignments relating to what you think of your man's penis.

15% of the BJ Woes is the visualization you give him. Your excitement when doing him and your willingness to practice mastering your techniques will heighten his sensation. Not being afraid to be touched, looked at or communicated with will enhance his erection, also. Don't forget his buddies (the ballz) and the sucking and slurping sounds. Combine that with him being able to move around and possibly play with your hair, your breast and/or Ms. Kitty (your vagina).

Most importantly, avoid making him feel uncomfortable as he watches you in a state of bliss. Looking at you give him oral sex is the ultimate visual for him. It's a man ego thing! *Just Go With It*! Become his fantasy - that will send him through the roof. Always use your most seductive weapon... Your Mind!

Now THAT'S Priceless

Chapter 2   I Can't Because...

Bring Out Your ORAL Diva
Should I OR Shouldn't I

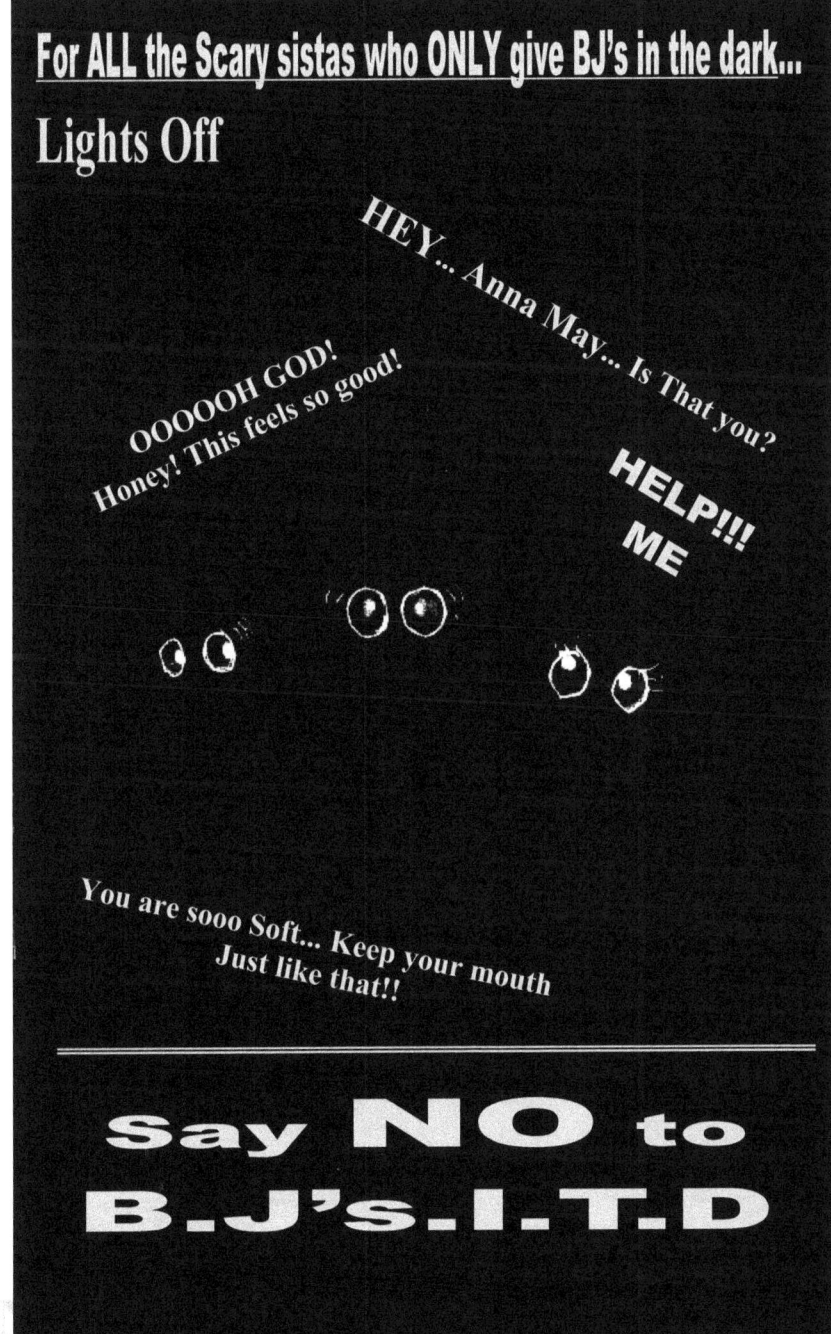

Fixable Dilemmas and Solutions

Bring Out Your ORAL Diva

Should I OR Shouldn't I

His penis doesn't look right... He's not circumcised!

Is that *really* the reason!? That's equivalent to the trust issue. You knew he wasn't circumcised *before* the Oral Sex dilemma, and yet, you *still* chose to get with him. I assume you've had sex with him already and if that wasn't an issue then, it shouldn't be a reason not to perform Oral Sex on him now. Don't *not* do a brotha over his natural skin that *every* man was born with. Every mammal was born with some type of foreskin (glans protection) - is nature wrong or is it our thinking?

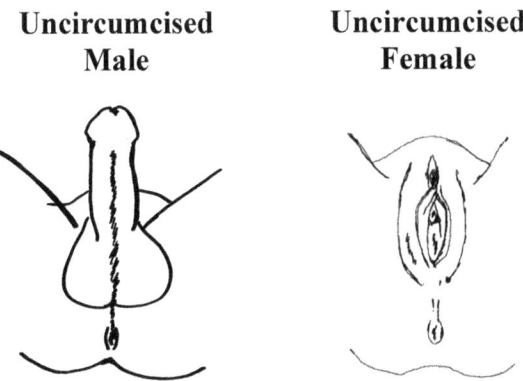

Now, this is what the male and female anatomy looks like.

Fixable Dilemmas and Solutions

Side be side, the genitalia, including the anus, are aligned in the same area. We are the same. Start looking at your man's body, especially from the waist down, as a beautiful piece of art—not something made of snails, puppy dog tails or something that has to be altered from its natural state.

Just as Oral Sex and sex in general, we tend to take the same steps as our parents. Our parents were wrong and misinformed about sex and circumcision; this should not be the reasons that you repeat the same cycles that didn't work in the past.

I can write a book alone about foreskin versus no foreskin. I will say this, Americans have the highest number of babies being circumcised; and yet, there are more uncircumcised males in the world. They do just fine with their foreskin. The man that is *not* circumcised is more sensitive around the head, thus possibly, cuming faster during Oral Sex. That can be a plus for you.

> **Interesting Info**
> Circumcision is *not* part of having a baby boy, anymore. Many hospitals don't do it; now, it's considered cosmetic surgery. AND the foreskin is not disregarded; it's used for different things. You are wearing it on your face and body. Foreskin comes in forms
> of facial crèmes and other cosmetics because of the collagen and it's cheaper for companies to get, but you pay top dollar for it.
> **So leave the foreskin where it belongs, protecting the penis AND NOT in a jar**
> Resource: Manswers

Chapter 2   I Can't Because...

Bring Out Your ORAL Diva
Should I OR Shouldn't I

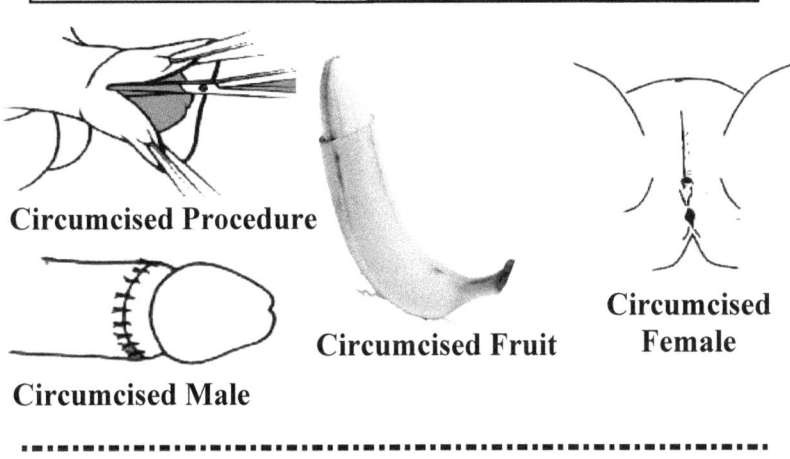

> When did *natural* start looking unnatural to us?
> **You alter nature...** You alter its function

Circumcised Procedure

Circumcised Male

Circumcised Fruit

Circumcised Female

I am sure you can tell my stance about circumcision of any kind, unless medically necessary. Whatever your man has, foreskin or no foreskin, is big or small, has hair or is hairless... it doesn't matter! No one should have to *permanently* alter their body to make it acceptable for someone else. You are not going to change anything, so get over it. To get info on circumcised versus uncircumcised and the most sensitive parts of the penis, read the chapter about the **Anatomy of Your Man.**

> To get all the info about circumcision, visit
> www.nocirc.org &
> www. VSGseries.com

Fixable Dilemmas and Solutions

His balls and dick smell musty and I will get sick

So fixable! If I got a quarter every time I heard women say this, I would be rich. If I got a quarter for all the times I've heard men say the same thing about us (women), I would be richer. The truth of the matter is, everyone has a natural body odor—and then... there's *funk*.

The Sudoriferous/Eccrine gland produces odorless perspiration (sudor/sweat) to cool down your body's temperature. Sweat tends to become kind of funky because of the germs and bacteria on the skin mixing together in those little naturally moist areas where the skin constantly rubs up against itself. Now, if your man is requesting a blow job immediately after playing his favorite sport for two hours or he hasn't bathed in the last 24-48 hours, then I can see your point.

The other type of perspiration/sweat is from the Apocrine gland. This gland produces a natural sexual scent called *pheromones*. These pheromones attract the opposite sex, and this seductive scent is more concentrated in the armpits and genital area. Now, if he is requesting a blow job within an hour after bathing and had no heavy perspiration producing activity beforehand, nor does he suffer from bromodrosis, this could be simply pheromones that you smell. That isn't necessarily a bad thing, we pay more money for things that have chemically made pheromones in it. If you can't tell the difference nor do you care to...

YOU'RE STILL JUST SCURED!!

The moment we get out of the shower, we start to perspire because of the temperature changes and quick body movements. So, although you put on your smell good, as soon as you start walking and moving around, those little areas get moist and rub together, producing funk. Honestly, everyone loses freshness within 1 hour or so in those naturally smelly areas. They include:

- the inner and outer part of the vulva (the vagina)
  the bushier, the smellier
- the inner part of the buttocks (the crack)
  men and women have hair in the crease of the buttocks and inner part of the thighs. If you don't shave that area off or down, the smellier it is
- underneath the breast
- under any rolls of skin
- the armpits
- between/under the toes

Fixable Dilemmas and Solutions

- the crease in the inner thighs, by the genitals
- underneath the penis and the scrotum
- behind the ears
- inside the navel

What most women don't realize is that the hair and scalp are very smelly, especially if you don't shampoo more often than once a week. Braids and weave gets noticeably smelly after a while, and that doesn't stop your man from taking you out, eating you out or wearing you out. I prefer you hear the smelly truth from me, your *Village Sista Girlfriend*, then to assume men don't have the same complaints about us as we do about them. The only difference for the man is, in many cases, that's not a good enough reason to deny you oral pleasure.

It is in your best interest that the *both* of you take a shower or wash your hands and those other specific areas thoroughly before Oral Sex or intercourse. Also, make sure the both of you wash your hands after oral sex, too. We have over 4,000 types of germs on our hands at any given moment and on any given day. If he's touching your vagina and stimulating the clitoris, guess who has a higher chance of getting an infection?

Chapter 2   I Can't Because...

Bring Out Your ORAL Diva
Should I OR Shouldn't I

> If your man is funky and/or musty, take a shower together. Or simply say,
> "Hey bebe! I want you smellin fresh, so I can suck you dry!"

After you say the statement above, he will eagerly jump up and disinfect his dick with bleach, dip his balls in hot boiling water and scrape off his pubic hair with a steel Brillo pad - just keep your promise and give him head. If him being clean is all that he has to do to receive that awesome blow job from you... get your mouth ready!

> **Now,**
> **when your man is officially sanitized, now what!?**
> **Many of us will find *another* reason not to do it.**
> **<u>So that really wasn't the problem.</u>**

Fixable Dilemmas and Solutions

Watch your words, Sista - WE are at war!

'What you won't do', there's so many sistas that will! When I say this, I am not trying to threaten or pressure you into doing anything. I am simply stating a fact. When I say this to some sistas, they appear to be insulted by the statement. They have that typical angry nonchalant attitude with the words to match "*O Well*! Then he can go right ahead!" Many sistas act as if they are not concerned over the possibility of their man receiving Oral Sex from another woman. That "*O Well*" can kick off life changing moments you never thought were possible.

I would never say anything to put fear in your heart; I just want you to know the truth - there's really no such thing as *surprises* in a troubled relationship. There's no one who is blameless in a failed relationship, nor does the *it just happened* theory exists in successful ones.

In relationships, there's the hidden game of war. Most women who nonchalantly say things they cannot come back from (like the "*O Well*! Then he can go right on ahead!") do not realize the war that they are in. You are at war with people you don't even realize… you are losing the war to the other sistas that *will*.

Chapter 2   I Can't Because...

Bring Out Your ORAL Diva
Should I OR Shouldn't I

Description of the Sista That Will

Myth: Some sistas think brothas only get blow jobs from hypes, busdowns, hoodrats or someone considered to be of substandard quality. Nor does a man receive Oral Sex from a person just one time or with your permission. This is so far from the truth.

The sista that will tends to favor you a lot, she's 'Holden IT Down' just like you... doesn't need a man... just like you. BUT the difference is she appreciates *your* man more than you do. Her list of sexual NO's is a lot shorter than yours, and she realizes your man ain't as bad as you make him out to be. She greets him with smiles and says hello, not with the frowns and attitudes you have been giving him as of late. She wants him for more than just a one time blow job and eagerly waits for you to push him away while she tries to move in for the kill. And trust me, your man is probably goin down town on her and hittin it from the front, the back with the protection called **LUCK** (not FDA approved). He actual loves you, but it just feeeeels so good to be wanted!

The saddest part is she favors you because you like her, too. Your man might have spoken about her to you a time or two, Beware of the hidden enemies, your friends, people that your man spend a lot of private time with and his co workers.

Don't blame her solely - you told her to when you proudly boosted about what you would *never* do - you gave your permission with the
"O WELL! Then he can just go right ahead"

Fixable Dilemmas and Solutions

I don't want to kiss my kids if I do something like that

Your kids have nothing to do with your sex life. You must not use your children as scapegoats; these are your own insecurities. The mouth and hands are the dirtiest part of the body; and yet, we use them both for foreplay and feeding our kids. Based on your own theory that fluids last forever, you still have the love juices on your body from your first sexual encounter. If what you say is true, he probably has your juices on his mouth and still he has gone down on you without your concerns of him kissing the kids. And yet, I have never heard a woman say, "I don't want my man to kiss or touch me or my kids after making love" or "don't do the dishes or help around the house because my fluids might be on your hands." Natural fluids do not stay in your mouth for hours, days or years. Your mouth makes new saliva every second.

This is so fixable... Brush YOUR Teeth!! Rinse Out YOUR Mouth!! **Wash your hands! Go On With Your Oral Lives!**

First, bodily fluids such as saliva, sweat, body oil, semen or vaginal fluids are naturally produced by your body under normal circumstances and won't make you sick. Semen is not bacteria or a virus and if you practice proper hygiene, this should not be an issue. If this is still an issue, just think about all the times your man went down on you and kissed you with no problems. Has your man ever kissed his children and they had to be rushed to the doctor because of the Oral Sex he performed on you? NO!

Stop Making Excuses!

Anytime you kiss and touch your children's hands, mouth, nose or eyes for any reason, you are passing germs that can possibly get them sick. And yet, your kids have no problem with their health. Most people don't kiss their children immediately after a lovemaking session, and I don't know of anyone that performed Oral Sex on someone and as soon as she/he got up, sex juice dripping from her/his mouth and fingers… she/he immediately went to kiss their child. It sounds gross and simply unrealistic, so why must you visualize something so disturbing and torment yourself with the thought of something that won't happen.

Ask yourself, what do you possibly think will happen to your mouth/body after Oral Sex and you have brushed your teeth afterwards?

Fixable Dilemmas and Solutions

Assignment

What's the worst that can happen? Write it down, challenge yourself and write it in the Forum so you will get answers and see your progress.

Scan for forums

___

If you cannot find a remedy for this matter, E-mail me with your concerns and the Village can find a solution that will work for the both of you.
www.VSGseries.com

(click on) the list of ***Most Common Reasons Not To Give Head;*** voice your concern and you can leave your e-mail for a response back.

Assignment/Homework

Small Steps equals Big Success
NOT Forbidden

After you have written down one reason, use the coupons below to work on your fears. The Comfy Coupon puts the control in your hands and the icing on his cake will be you becoming comfortable with performing oral sex and stroking his penis beforehand, as you initiate what will happen between the two of you. Here is one complimentary coupon as an example. Fill out the other one your way. If still in doubt, ask for assistance on V.S.G. Facebook or email me your dilemma and see if the village can help.

Be realistic! Don't sabotage the moment by suggesting something he's not in to or purposely pick a date that's not convenient for the both of you. This is your moment to conquer a fear on your terms.

Comfy Coupons ™

Booklet of ideas coming soon - check online * Join our email list

---

Date of offer: _____   TO: _ _ _ _ _ _ _ _ _ _

Lets: **Listen to our favorite music as we go to sleep and stroke and kiss each other and cume from it**

Goal: For both of us to cume from hand jobs for starters

Comfy Coupons ™   www.villagesistagirlfriend.com

Date of offer: _____   TO: _ _ _ _ _ _ _ _ _ _

Lets: _____

_____

Goal: _____

Comfy Coupons ™   www.villagesistagirlfriend.com

Assignment/Homework

I don't want him to cume in my mouth

It is reasonable to feel this way about the *cumming in your mouth* thing. We have been so traumatized about Oral Sex that swallowing anything enjoyable that's creamy or white can be an embarrassment for you. Even licking on an ice-cream cone, on a hot summer day, in public, will have some sistas looking around in fear of who's watching and what they might think.

Ask yourself, *"Why is his cumming in my mouth a big issue?"*

I have listened to women give all types of reasons, from being allergic to semen, their throat closing up, to vomiting/gagging uncontrollably and the classic "I think giving him a blow job is enough! He better be glad he gets it on more than one holiday."

Fixable Dilemmas and Solutions

First, let's get the vital information:

When you think of a man's cume - what does it remind you of? (ex: sweetness, monkey snot, etc.) _____

List at least 4 names/things you think of a man's cume

1. _____ 2. _____

3. _____ 4. _____

When you think of **_your man's cume_**, is the description any different than the above? If so, what are they?

1. _____

2. _____

3. _____

4. _____

If your words were that of disgust and would make a person want to vomit or when you envision the *white* stuff coming out, you become visibly sick, like now, it is understandable why you feel the way you do about Oral Sex.

> I won't even think about talking about swallowing... YET!!

Assignment/Homework

Bring Out Your ORAL Diva
Should I OR Shouldn't I

Don't Forget

go online and join the Village. Our goal is to have it completely up and running very soon. This will be a sista's resource for everything. And, if you'd like, book a party for you and a couple of your closest lady friends and learn even more on this topic. If you can gather some of your married friends, we'll have an education on how to love one another better.

www.VSGseries.com

Join the email list for various blogs, polls and forums.

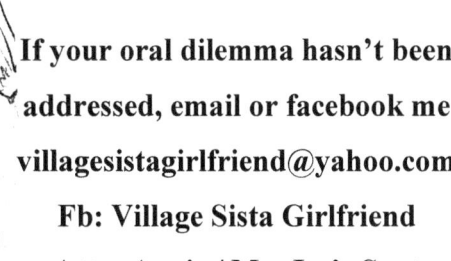

If your oral dilemma hasn't been addressed, email or facebook me

villagesistagirlfriend@yahoo.com

Fb: Village Sista Girlfriend

Attn: Angie / Mz. Jee's Spot

Share your knowledge with the rest of us

Fixable Dilemmas and Solutions

www.VSGseries.com
Change Starts with YOU... Right NOW!

Take the Test:

Are You a Negative Sucker
(check ✓ all that apply)

☐ Roll your eyes or sighs when he reluctantly asks you for some head on his birthday

☐ Ask him *is his dick clean* before you go down on him

☐ Become instantly irritated if he touches you, looks at you, turn the lights on, moves for any reason, enjoys the blow job, even when *you* don't

☐ You stop if he makes any sounds resembling pleasure

☐ Complain about your chronic neck pain when it's time to do him

☐ Your erotic Oral Sex sounds consist of choking, gagging, hacking up tiny bits of pubic hair and stopping because you swear your throat closes up every time his penis touches your lips

Assignment/Homework

Small Steps equals Big Success
NOT Forbidden

TEST

☐ When he tries to tell you what he wants orally, you instantly get on the defensive and say "All the *other* men I've been with didn't need all *this* to get hard."

☐ Your list of Don'ts is 10x's longer than your list of Do's

☐ After he waited and begged you for weeks, you're finally forced to go down on him as he hums the theme song from the game show *Jeopardy*. You make it very clear you don't like this dick suckin thing as you *accidentally* scrape his dick with your teeth… over and over and over again. He loses his erection… and you say "What's Wrong With *YOU*!"

If you checked off *anyone* of these…

Assignment/Homework

You are a Negative Sucker

You must go to Dickology 101 * Beginners Class

Y'all made me late again for Dickology 101!
My man said don't come home til I get the certificate
that shows him
I graduated with the highest honors

Chapter 2 I Can't Because...

To Swallow OR *NOT* To Swallow
The plot thickens

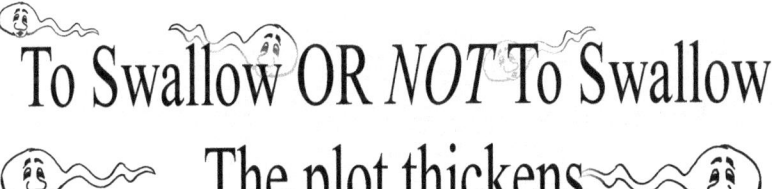

Chapter 3

Self Help

Here are some common concerns I have answered about swallowing sperm over the years

1. Is Sperm/Semen safe to digest!?

Under normal circumstances, cume is safe for you to digest. If your man does not have any diseases or infections, his semen or sperm doesn't have anything like that in it either. If you sincerely thinks he has a STD, that is a justifiable reason why you shouldn't go down on him, but if that is what you're thinking, then why are you *still* with him? I hope you realize whatever he has, you already have it vaginally, if you're having unprotected sex with him.

If you choose to be with a man who has a STD and you practice safe sex, that still applies to Oral Sex. You must use a condom and dental dams (for women). They can help prevent fluid from entering your mouth, but understand that these items don't protect you from everything. Being in a relationship with someone who has a STD, knowingly or unknowingly, is not as uncommon as one think.

> **Note:**
> Having sex with someone and not knowing their STD status happens all the time. Just go online and type *'celebrities with STDs'*.

Chapter 3   YOU Can DO THIS

> If you feel your man has a STD and you've been saying that for years, but has never done anything about it - Face It, that's simply your excuse you use not to do it.

As far as medication is concerned, I've researched and could not find the amount of medication that remains in semen or in our vaginal fluid, for that matter. I don't know of any female that suffered from complications of swallowing due to a man's medication. Sperm/Semen is not deadly to your body, no matter what your *girls* say. Nor have I heard of a woman tell a man not to eat her out because of her concern for his safety in regards to her birth control pills, estrogen pills or all the other medications she takes.

Nor have I heard of a man having to go to the doctor after eating out his woman. If your man has cume inside/on you, and you did not suffer an allergic reaction, you shouldn't have anything to worry about. You do not have to get your stomach pumped afterwards and no one can tell if you've swallowed! And if they could… So What! That's your man…

Your Relationship... Your Business!

Self Help

Interesting info:

* Currently, Chlamydia is the most common STD.

* 40%, nearly 1 in 2, of those who are sexually active are suspected carriers of Chlamydia.

* 2/3 of the people in the United States, under the age of 25 will have a STD in their lifetime.

* 1 in 2 people who are sexually active between the ages of 15-24 have a STD.

* 1 in 5 Americans over the age of 12 have genital herpes.

* 1 in 4 women have genital herpes. There is no cure for herpes 2.

* 75% (more than half) of the reproductive population is infected with HPV (genital warts). There is no cure for HPV 3.

* 1 in 250 Americans has AIDS. AIDS is the 6th leading cause of death among persons 15-24 years of age and 20% are infected during the teen years. There is no cure for AIDS.

> After reading the grim facts,
> I can't stress enough, make it your mission to get out of the *friends with benefits* or *dip on the side* department; it can shorten your life.

Rule #1

Every man that you get involved with must have the potential to be your huzband.

This rule will make it easier for you to give oral sex to the man you are with - the one you love

If you are in a relationship, your goal is to do whatever it takes *between the two* of you to help with each other's happiness. YEP!

That includes a lil Sucky Sucky!

2. I am allergic to sperm/semen because I feel my throat closing up when I am giving Oral Sex; especially when he is about to cume.

The mind is a powerful thing. If you think that's what will happen… then it will! Many women would love to tell their man they have a legitimate medical condition that hinders them from doing this *suckin* and *swallowin* thing. Actually, there is a condition that can affect your swallowing.

The technical term is called **Dysphagia.**

You might have Dysphagia if you suffer from any of the following

(check all that apply)
- Caustic esophagitis
- Head or neck cancer
- Webs
- Goiter
- Cervical osteophytes
- Zenker diverticulum
- Post-surgical/radiation
- Stenosis (narrowing)
- Infections (tonsilar enlargement/abscess)
- *Neurogenic*
- Multiple sclerosis
- Stroke

Your ORAL Diva
Should I OR Shouldn't I

- Head injury
- Alzheimer's disease
- Parkinson's disease
- Brain tumor

If you checked nothing... that's fantastic...

You're just Scured – and that's *FIXABLE*

People with some forms of Dysphagia suffer from various eating disorders. Also, people who suffer from this illness tend to be extremely underweight and malnourished because they have a problem swallowing everything. Some don't swallow *anything* at all - no liquids, including water or even their own saliva. I saw a lady on T.V. that had to eat from a feeding tube that was surgically inserted in her stomach. She was terrified to let anything go down her throat. She was sexually abused, for years, by her best friend's father as a child. There was nothing physically wrong with her throat... it was all mental.

> If you are a thick, solid food eatin sista, who finishes a full course meal with some libations (liquids); it's safe to say you don't have to tell your man the bad news (for you), you can't swallow due to this condition. If you enjoy long deep tongue and saliva filled kisses from your man then
> ### Stop Prayin that you have Dysphagia...
> ### YOU KNOW YOU DON'T

Self Help

3. How does it (sperm/semen/nut) taste?

Unrealistic Thoughts

Self Help

Yummy! Tastes Like Chicken!

This swallowing thing is drastically overrated. First, semen is made up of fructose (sugars), some vitamins, proteins and a lot of other technical stuff that's not important to you unless you are a scientist. Semen has a slight alkaline base of about 7.2-8.0. It's not acidic like vinegar. So there goes the myth of semen tasting extremely bitter. And there is not enough fruit in the world that will make semen taste like pineapples or cherries; so stop putting your man on a six-month fruit diet... *it doesn't work*!

You have to be realistic, how many brothas do you know that will change their *entire* eating habits, in order to get *a blow job* on his birthday... *maybe*!? What makes you so different from the women of his past? You see he loves you and you know it; but do you think he feels good about this part of the relationship, especially when he has never had to change his eating habits for blow jobs before? And, if by some miracle, he did go on your fruit diet, you would still only do it on your terms—when you *feel* like it. Your dilemma really isn't the taste. Mentally, you have not accepted Oral Sex completely as being OK.

I'm tellin you. you really can't taste anything! You should have so much saliva in your mouth—it is going directly down your throat... there's nothing to taste. You only have taste buds on the tips and sides of the tongue, so if you just swallow without *purposely* trying to taste anything, you shouldn't have a problem. The times that I could taste something, it wasn't anything that stood out in my mind as tasting horrible. Unless you swish his semen around in your mouth, like a fine wine... you really shouldn't be able to taste anything.

Women debate back and forth about what a man's cume looks like. I hear women say sperm smells nasty and it's super thick. They give a visual description, like it smells like bleach, it is as thick as peanut butter and clumpy stuff is in it. I've heard, he cumes so much, it's like swallowing an 8oz cup full of nut. It's simply not true! If your man's cume smells like bleach, is thick and clumpy like crunchy peanut butter and he shoots an 8oz cup full of nut...

Self Help

Drop The Book! Immediately call 911...
something ain't right!

His cume does not shoot out like a speeding bullet that will put your eye out. You can actually feel the pulsation of his penis (the urethra) before he is about to cume. It's really no surprise; you can mentally prepare yourself to swallow his sweet juices, long before you even have to. The average man's cume is slightly over a teaspoon and the consistency is equivalent to the texture of honey.

I have met many women that do not swallow, and I've also met many women that proudly do. I am not saying swallowing is the cure to your relationship woes, but how can you want someone that goes down on you with no restrictions, swallows you all the time without the attitude, and you expect him to enjoy *and* accept *ALL* your restrictions. Yeah! I want a flying unicorn too. **(So Unrealistic)**

Chapter 3   **YOU Can DO THIS**

Should I OR Shouldn't I

Ladies, I must tell you something I know you don't want to hear. "We do not taste like peaches & cream or cherries!" I couldn't believe it myself! How can I not taste sweet and juicy? My man makes me feel like I'm the best dessert he's ever had in his life! He makes me feel like I taste better than his mom's cooking.

I am blushing, flattered and erotically tingling when he licks his fingers afterward and says "hmmmmm that was soooo good!" "Wooooow!" His words are an aphrodisiac to my soul. My body still quivers as he licks the very last drop of me. I can't wait to give him the same pleasure. Orally bringing him to ecstasy is my mission because I know he loves doing whatever it takes to please me too.

Your man licks you like a lollipop, sucks on you like a sweet juicy peach and swallows your creamy goodness, simply because turning you on is the ultimate turn on to him. I'm turned on myself as I think about being compared to the taste of lollipops, sweet juicy peaches and creamy goodness. Women tasting delicious is a common theme in many songs.

Self Help

Disliking him and how he taste started in Pre-K... when you were learning your ABC's and nursery rhymes such as:

> **What are little girls made of?**
> **"Sugar and spice and all things nice**
> **That's what little girls are made of"**

> **What are little boys made of?**
> **"Snips and snails, and puppy dogs tails**
> **That's what little boys are made of"**

Arthur unknown

I don't hear this nursery rhyme being said much anymore, but if you're 25 and older, you have probably heard it. The mental damage is already done. Based on this nursery rhyme, which person (boy/girl) sound deliciously sweet and tasty? I am convinced that is one of the reasons why it is so easy for women to accept being eaten out. We think that we are some how tastier than a man, and therefore, it should be an honor when we allow him the pleasure of licking and sucking our cherry.

Chapter 3   **YOU Can DO THIS**

Now, the real truth is, there's not much of a difference between male and female. There's less than 10% of a anatomical difference that becomes noticeable when we (girls & boys) hit puberty and the hormones alter our appearance. But technically, we are the same from the head down to our toenails. Down from our sweat to other bodily fluids, the ph is the same and does the same for a man or a woman. A man doesn't taste sour while a woman tastes sweet. You can't tell the difference between the female and male genitalia in the early part of pregnancy because we are made of the same things.

This is what the genitalia looks like in the early trimester of pregnancy. Which one is male or female? This is color coded. Notice what each one of the parts become.

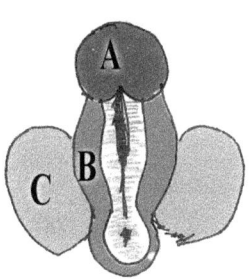 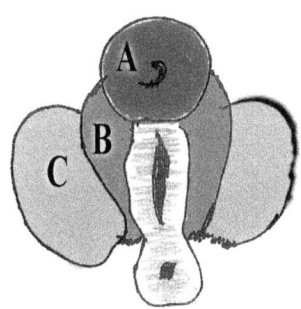

Which one is male? Which one is female?
Where is the penis? Where the clitoris?

Self Help

The Penis At 8 weeks

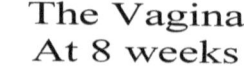
The Vagina At 8 weeks

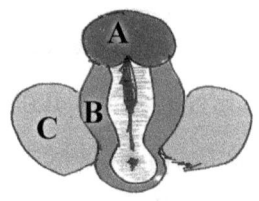
The Penis At birth

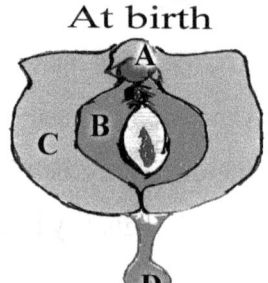
The Vagina At birth

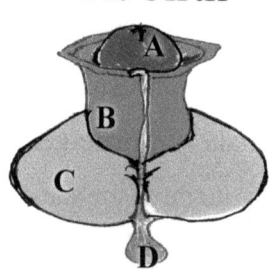

<u>A</u>   becomes the penis glan & coronal ridge of the penis and that same area becomes the clitoris of the vagina. Both has an abundance of nerve endings.

<u>B</u>   becomes the foreskin of the penis and this also becomes the labia of the vagina.

<u>C</u>   becomes the scrotum of a male and the labia majora of a female. Even the <u>anus</u> <u>D</u> is in the same place for both.

Everything is in the same place and has the same structure. There's no snails or puppy dog tails or sugar and spices. We are only different by the X or Y chromosome, and that's less than a 10 percent difference between us.

> **your man is sucking on the same things that he expects you to suck on.**

Chapter 3   YOU Can DO THIS

Some of the *Real Reasons* why you have a problem with Oral Sex

1. Mentally, you are still suffering from the *good girl syndrome* and doing this, you feel is the ultimate betrayal to your parents and how you were raised.

2. You are afraid of what he might think and what you might think of yourself afterwards. If it feels good to you - you feel guilty because you've been taught that only *bad* girls enjoy this.

3. Doing this (Oral Sex and swallowing) might make you love him more then you want to because you consider this the ultimate thing to do as a sign of everlasting love.

4. In the back of your mind, you are concerned about what others might think of you versus the satisfaction of your man and having a better relationship between the two of you.

5. You might start questioning everything you were told if you force yourself to come face-to-face with the fact that many of the things you were told about sex, Oral Sex (something that parents never talked about) by the people you love were simply half-truths, myths and some were just downright lies.

Self Help

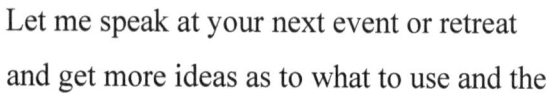

If you are interested in learning more:

Let me speak at your next event or retreat and get more ideas as to what to use and the ***How To's on Everything.***

> Go online and join our email list
> for the tools you need
> to be a better lover

Just as I have given many reasons as to why women say they don't want to give head, here are some of the reasons many women, like myself, love to.

OOOH! The Benefits of Giving GREAT Head

Women that give unrestricted great head will get the same in return. It's no secret, great sex and a great relationship goes hand and hand. He is less likely to act like it's just him in the bedroom and cume in a second. When a man knows you care about his sexual satisfaction, he will care about your satisfaction, too. This *'I will give what I expect attitude'* will keep you in a healthy relationship.

Being able to satisfy your lover in this way can be a major turn on for you. Unfortunately, some sistas think that Oral Sex is unnecessary. What is truly unnecessary, are the restrictions women knowingly put upon their relationship that is guaranteed to do more harm than good. Sistas boast about being a great mom, a great cook, a great follower of their religion, but I never hear a sista boast about her relationship with the man she chose to stay involved with or married. Can you boast about being a great unselfish partner!? I can, do and will *every* chance I get, and I know my man is the envy amongst some of the fellas because of it. And some sistas hate me for it. **"*SO What* - Let the Hater's Hate" says Coty Cash.**

It is a fun sex act and/or is the ultimate foreplay for your man. You can start off with a hand job as his moist tongue circles your harden nipples or he can stroke your clitoris. Fun sex includes both partners exploring each other's body. *Remember,* foreplay is being turned on before the sexual act, not anticipating being unsatisfied and then expecting to perform.

Oral Sex can keep your man erect longer. Before he cumes, you can orally stimulate the shaft and delay his climax by not focusing on the coronal ridge. When you are in tune with his body, in most cases, you can tell when he is about to cume. During Oral Sex, if

OOOH! The Benefits of Giving GREAT Head

you are looking up at him, you can talk him through maintaining his erection in a seductive way where he will almost cume on command. You are developing your *Ultimate Oral Diva Skills*.

As your man gets older, Oral Sex is the key to his harden erection and longevity. No different than the foreplay needed to get you started and needed to keep you going, he needs continuous foreplay, also. Although many sistas will disagree, your man needs more than just an invitation to the bedroom from you. Lingerie, although sexy, won't keep him rock hard long, unless you are doing other things, like oral foreplay. In the end, you benefit the most from giving him oral.

If a rock hard penis is your preference, this is the way to get it. If you start off with oral, he can be harder and last longer because all his nerve endings are being stimulated. The icing on his cake is the woman he loves is blowing both his minds - *at the same times*. After a little oral foreplay, his hard penis thrusting deep inside you can send him (and you) on cloud nine.

If he gets soft in the middle of the sex act, don't worry, just give him head and he can get started again. Sometimes, a man loses his firmness during sex; it does not mean that he has been cheating; he just needs more direct stimulation from you at various time during the lovemaking session - YEP! Oral Sex.

OMG! Who knew you could be turned on by your man's monstrous face, curled toes, spasmed body and sounds that would scare you out of your wits if it was heard during any other occasion. If you have never made your man cume this way, you have truly missed out. Don't worry, I can sense your mind opening up - you'll see his monster face soon.

This is one of the reasons why your man loves eating you out. Your orgasms are more intense from oral sex. And he knows this. When he envisions your face when you orgasm from oral sex, trust me, he's erect from the thought. When you make this happen, you will get turned on envisioning him and what you have done - every time.

Although Janet Jackson probably didn't mean it this way but *Control* **is an awesome** feeling you get when you are able to satisfy your man in *every* way... especially orally. He is at your mercy for about five to seven seconds, as you give him pleasures that only you, the one he cares about, can give.

I have met women in the beginning of a party that say they don't give head and soon see them leave with an open mind after the education. Months later, I've heard some of these women gloat about receiving a lot more great gifts from their guy because they have become great at their oral craft. Women who have no Oral Sex dilemma laugh about how some of their extra bills get paid. Now,

OOOH! The Benefits of Giving GREAT Head

I don't promote blow jobs in exchange for money, but *ain't nothing wrong with nicer gifts and a good credit score.* The philosophy behind this is, *"keep your man happy, and he will keep you the happiest."* Happiness is more than just the dinner you cook for him. He will enjoy your dinner a whole lot more if you let him be your dinner sometimes.

Why not *Just Because* you love him and you are into each other? You know that's something he wants from you. So many sistas accept being the dip on the side and give their heart, body and soul to a brotha that doesn't think twice about them. It would be great if I could use the word *love* in this book, every time I mentioned Oral Sex. If I did, that would give some ladies an excuse to justify their selfish ways along with unrealistic expectations. Wake Up, Sista! No matter what the *world* says, realize you got a man! It should be your priority to keep him. You must be willing to keep love new and an open mind to trying new things between the two of you. Remember, love is what keeps you willing to try to make it work. **"You must motivate yourself to change" says T.J Lawler.**

You see, I've also met women that have said they're not in love with their man, but be the mother of his children, have been living together for years and some are even married to the man they refuse to give oral to. Many of these sistas have bragged in front of other sistas about how little they give head – if any at all. That same sista would be insulted if her man didn't go down on her, but in the same breath, will say they have not been together long enough for him to receive oral. I have counseled married women, young and old, some at their bachelorette party and others that have been together, with the same man, for twenty plus years who have said the same thing...

"He has to prove himself first!"

So you see,
the majority of women don't change, even if they have been with their man for a month or decades. Although we have been taught by the world to quickly judge a brotha, we don't want to take responsibility for choosing him so we don't have to justify or stand behind the things we do.
It's hard to change, unless you feel you must.

If you are wondering...
What does this have to do
with a blow job?!

You'll be amazed at what an unsatisfied, oral sexless brotha will do!

OOOH! The Benefits of Giving GREAT Head

When It's All Said & Done

Fear and *our own mental hang ups* are the reasons why we choose not to satisfy our man in that way.

Oral Sex within itself is not dangerous; you don't get sick from it, and it can be very enjoyable if you mentally are into it.

The truth is, it is simply another expression of the act of lovemaking when you are in a serious relationship with someone.

Unfortunately, as we become sexual women in committed relationships, we still make the choice to stick by the mis-education of our youth and can't understand how our relationships suffer as a result.

Oral Sex and good sex won't make a bad man good, but it will keep a good man happy and you would be missed big time
if he made the mistake and
F#@KED UP!

Chapter 5: Anatomy of Your Man

In order for you to be great at Oral Sex, you must know the *ins* and *outs* of your man's penis. Some ladies have the best intentions, but when it takes hand cramping, lockjaw and a stiff neck in order for him to *almost* cume, it's easy to see why you don't want to.

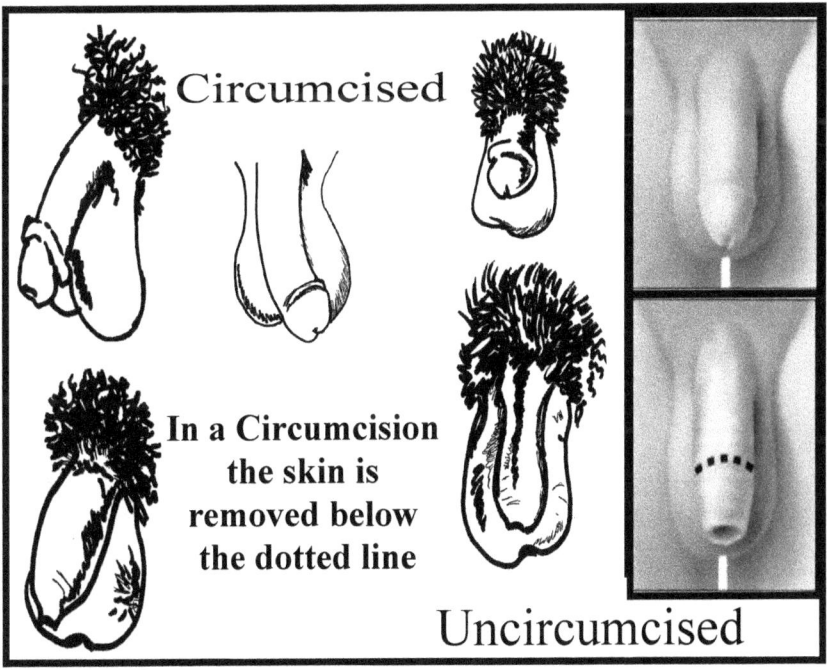

Circumcised

In a Circumcision the skin is removed below the dotted line

Uncircumcised

Look at these beautiful pieces of candy and artwork

Anatomy of Your Man

Circle the part of the penis *you* think is the *Most* sensitive?

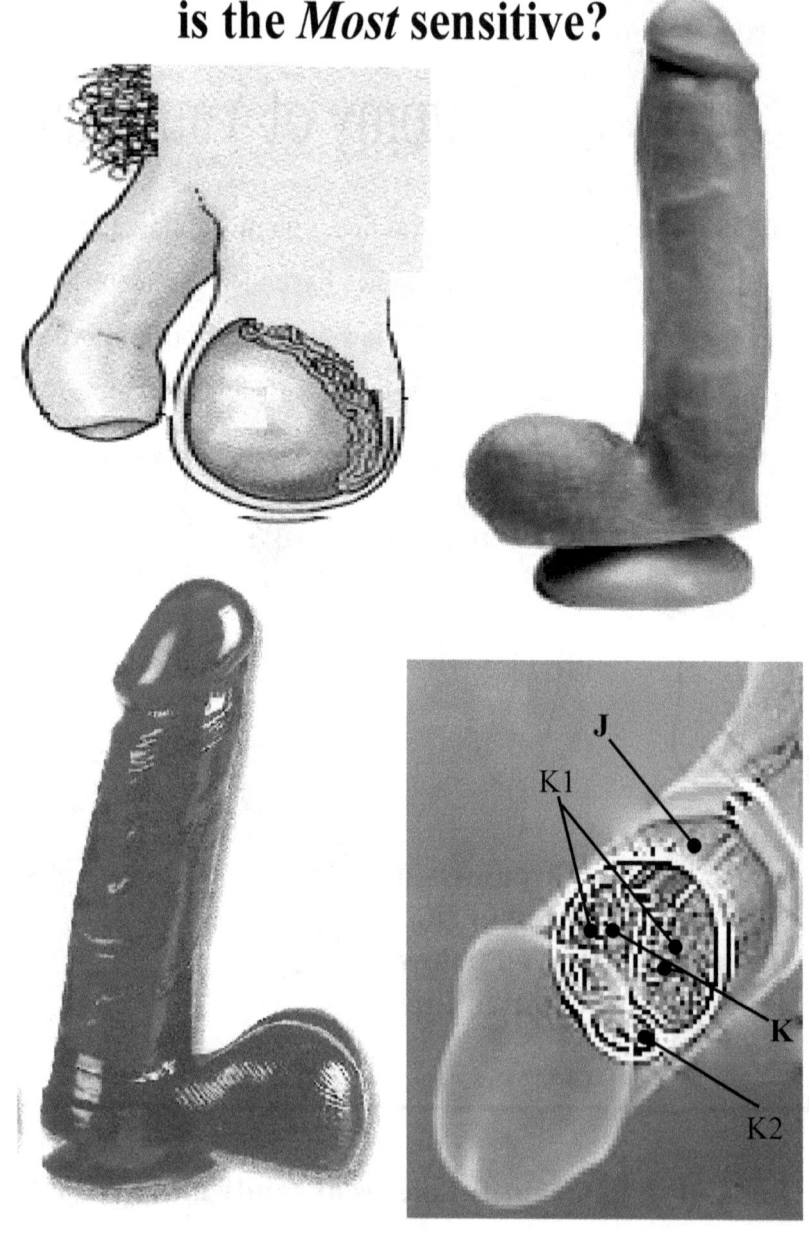

Chapter 5   **Learning the Ins and Outs**

Parts of the Penis

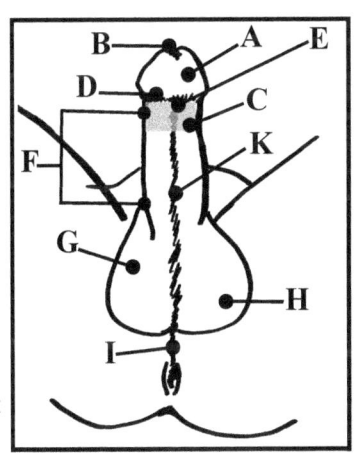

A. **Head (glans):** what you call the head up to the coronal ridge.

B. **Urethra opening (Meatus)**

C. **Foreskin (Gray Area):** that beautiful skin that has an abundance of nerve endings that keeps the head of the penis soft and clean. When he's erect, intact foreskin allows for maximum erection and has protected the head so well, it keeps friction down when he enters inside you. He doesn't have this foreskin if he has been traditionally circumcised.

D. **Coronal ridge:** that little 3/4th of an inch surrounding the top of the shaft, but right below the head

E. **Frenulum:** connective tissue the connects the foreskin to the shaft

F. **Shaft:** this is what most ladies calls the penis

G. **Scrotum (Sac):** the soft pouch of skin that protects the balls

H. **Testicles (Balls):** inside the scrotum

I. **Perineum:** the hairless highly sensitive area between the balls and anus (butt)

J. **Dorsal Vein:** the vein that protrudes from the skin (on the top side of the penis) especially when he is erect

K. **Cavernous Artery:** you don't see it, but you feel the effects when he is rock hard. The Cavernous Artery supplies oxygen rich blood to the K1 **Corpus Cavernosum** and the K2 **Corpos Spongiosum**; it feels like a ridge along the bottom side of the penis that extends up the shaft. **K1 and K2 are shown on the prior page.**

Anatomy of Your Man

Most Sensitive Parts are:

C. Foreskin: (extremely sensitive if uncircumcised) light gray area - Intact foreskin is equivalent to about 5 inches of skin covered with thousands of sensory nerve endings. This extremely sensitive skin keeps the penis glans (head) super soft and protects the urinary opening. When the penis becomes erect, the foreskin expands to compensate for his erection, as a result, even a portion of the shaft is extremely sensitive to touch and temperature changes.

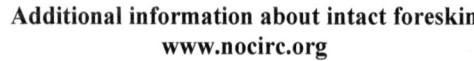

Additional information about intact foreskin
www.nocirc.org

D. Coronal Ridge: (most sensitive if circumcised or uncircumcised) dark gray area - Here you'll find the skin free of fat and full of nerve endings that lye very close to the surface of the penile skin; for this reason, this small area is super sensitive. Those *tiny little bumps below the Coronal Ridge* are extra sensitive when licked, so go for it. I said tiny bumps

NOT SORES
if you see sores anywhere,
call 911

E. Frenulum: (sensitive if uncircumcised) - This is the connective tissue that attaches the foreskin to the penis shaft and allows the foreskin to cover the (head) glans. If your man is circumcised, that connective tissue is missing with only a raised remnant on the surface on the underside of the head. If your man has been circumcised for some time, he has lost a lot of sensation. This is because when any part of the skin is constantly exposed to various climates and rubs against rough elements such as clothing or underwear you encounter some desensitization. Women have frenulums also.

Chapter 5   **Learning the Ins and Outs**

OMG - Oh MY Goodness! I almost forgot! The Ballz! Don't forget the Ballz! His penis and testicles are close friends. They are very sensitive when giving oral. It's a package deal. You can't just be on the ballz exclusively, and not give attention to the other sensitive parts. You must work on them all *simultaneously* in order for you to be at your best when giving head. Get ready to be a *Multitasker*.

Don't read ahead, but the Toe Curling *Tips & Techniques* Chapter 7 gives detail to help you orally multitask

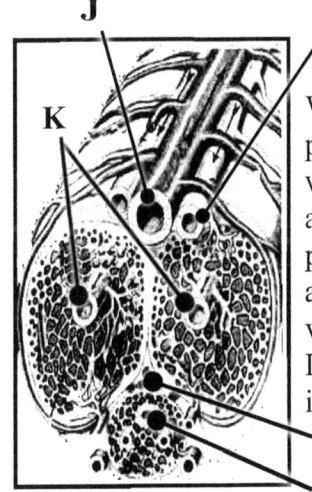

When I ask ladies about the most sensitive part of the penis, many have pointed to what they called *that* little artery. This actually runs along the entire length of the penis. What women point to is actually not an artery; it's called the Dorsal Vein. The vein itself feels no sensation. Although the Dorsal vein may not matter in his pleasure, it is essential in his erection.

Party Info

J. Dorsal vein: allows the normal break down of cell reproduction to be eliminated - *helps with his erection*

L. Dorsal artery: responsible for feeding rich blood to the skin and (head) glans - *help keeps the internal parts of the penis healthy*

M. Urethal artery: supply nourishment to the corpus spongiosum (erectile tissue) M1 the **Uretha opening**

K. Cavernous arteries: supply erectile tissue of the corpus Cavernosum (these creates the *hard* effect)

Anatomy of Your Man

His sensation is based on sensory nerves in the skin. To give you an idea how Oral Sex feels to him, gently rub your arm by your wrist. Now, gently rub the inner fold of your arm (the place where you've had blood drawn). The inner fold of the arm is extremely sensitive. Just like your man's coronal ridge, the skin sensitivity comes from the sensory nerves resting close on the skin's surface. This intense sensation is also magnified 100% because the skin is so thin in those areas. Now imagine a hot moist mouth, long slippery tongue, licking and sucking those sensitive areas. It feels AWESOME; it has nothing to do with you or how you were raised.

It simply feels fantastic to him

Chapter 5   **Learning the Ins and Outs**

Chapter 6

On Lubes & Stuff

If the taste of him, the pre-cume or his semen is your #1 problem, then your problem is **SOLVED**.

There are so many things to choose from that can make him taste better. Let's start off with the obvious.

Wash Up! The *both* of you! That can make a difference!

The Sticky Ickey of Things

Saliva (Spit)

Saliva is your natural tasteless lubricant. It's always there, ready to produce more when you need it. The good thing about saliva is you don't have to go looking for it in the dark. It is readily available and you can never run out.

Saliva, aka spit, is about 98% water and the rest of it is various proteins, enzymes and bacteria fighting agents. You can subconsciously affect how much saliva you produce during Oral Sex. Saliva itself doesn't smell bad; it's the bacteria in the mouth that produces bad breath. This is important to know because if you are not mentally ready to perform oral sex on him, you might not have enough saliva in your mouth to act as a lubricant, and that can lessen the oral/hand job experience OR you can be plagued with dry mouth and bad breath during the oral act. **That's so NOT Sexy!**

Some men are turned on or off by the spitting on the penis they see on TV. Ask your man, it matters. He will tell you if he wants you to spit on him. Just because he seems aroused by things doesn't mean he necessarily enjoy those things being done to him. When you watch porn movies, check out the blow job scenes. That big, long, two feet of endless white glob coming from the mouth of the one giving head is *not* just saliva. It is a combination of other things such as lubricants, oils, pre–cume, and other thickening agents. You must know that when it comes to porn movies, it is just that; *a movie*

Chapter 6

that is scripted and edited, along with retakes that include things that will make it look as if the actors are sucking and thrusting for hours. It's simply not true! And remember, the porn star has no problem with oral, so she can produce large amounts of saliva.

How can you produce more saliva naturally?

You must associate good thoughts with giving head/oral sex. Associate your favorite mouth watering desserts or drinks with his penis and the oral act. Shortly before the oral act, chew on things that are filled with natural juices, like cherries, peaches, oranges, cantaloupes, or a salad.

Suck on things that will get the salivary glands going, like ice and candy. Just stay away from things that are extremely sour or to sweet. If you chew or suck on things that already have a taste to it, this can help you not taste him as much. Honestly, if his penis (the skin) is clean, you don't taste anything. It may taste salty from sweat, but skin itself doesn't have a distinctive taste to it.

Lubricants aka Lube

My all time favorite are lubricants. Use one that is either water or silicone based. There are water/glycerin-based lubricants that natu-

The Sticky Ickey of Things

rally heat up with more friction. You can use any of these types of lubricants (water/silicone based) with condoms and dental dams.

My personal choice *now* is a non–flavored silicone based lubricant. A lil' silicone goes a long way. When I initially started educating myself and feeling comfortable about oral sex, I used a water based lube. The extreme gliding capabilities of the water based lube, made it seem like I was better (at oral sex and a hand job) than what I *really* was in the beginning. Water based lubes come in many flavors. If there is a fruit you love to eat, there is a lubricant out there that tastes like it. You take the lube and squeeze a nickel size amount in your hands or on top of his penis. Massage and stroke the lube over his entire penis and testicles. Use both hands, but let your writing hand lead; you have better control with stroking and gripping.

Another great thing I love about a silicone-based lube is that it instantly adjust to your body's temperature. Water-based lubes are at room temperature, so if it's cold, you feel the coldness on your skin for a couple of seconds. When it comes to price, silicone will cost more. But you literally only need a couple of drops, so in the end, it is very cost effective. Tasty flavored lubes can get the saliva glands going, thus making Oral Sex more enjoyable for you. Now you have the taste of your flavored fruit and your favorite man in your mouth, *at the same time*.

Chapter 6

If taste is not an issue, I recommend the one that has no flavor at all. I prefer lubes instead of just saliva alone; this combination helps my mouth and hands glide over the head, shaft and testicles a whole lot easier without the skin to skin friction. If you use a lube, it can cut your Oral Sex time down by 25-50%. Don't forget, with enough lubricant in your mouth, he can see a stream of love juice connecting your mouth to his penis like a pro.

Lubricants also can help with tired jaws, tired hands, dry mouth, and if you're not producing enough saliva throughout the Oral Sex session, you shouldn't give a blow job without it. The best thing about a lubricant, it can be used on you, too! Stroke him or do oral until he gets hard, the lube left on his penis, will make it easier to go inside you. And, if you are not wet and you are penetrated by your man's lubed penis... WHALA! You are super tight and that can feeeel soooo good for the *both* of you. Put it on his fingertips, guide his slippery fingers to your clitoris. His lubricated fingers will feel like silk as they glide back and forth over your erect nipples while you are performing Oral Sex on him.

Jellies & Creams

These are items that are geared specifically for making Oral Sex taste better. Many are thick and come in a variety of flavors. The purpose of the thickness is to coat your mouth and mask the taste of pre-cume or cume. They are great for giving your mouth a burst of flavor, but it isn't a lubricant. Some also have a minty taste so he can feel a little coolness/tingle (it's very little) as you are giving him oral pleasure. Before performing oral on him, you can place a nice amount of this type of jelly/cream on one fingertip, insert finger in your mouth, swish tongue around and KABOOM! He tastes great–less filling and you are ready to show off your Oral Diva skillz!

DT Sprays & Balms

This is great for all the gaggers and non swallowers. D.T. is short for deep throat desensitizing spray. Although they come in flavors, your throat is so numb, you can't taste the flavor. It is designed to numb your throat for a short period of time, so you can do what you need to do - deep throat and swallow! Some ladies pride themselves on vomiting, drooling and gagging uncontrollably on their man's penis... **That's *So NOT Sexy*!**

Benzocaine will become your best friend. This is the numbing agent found in many of your erectile sprays, vaginal and anal comfort products. These sprays and balms do just that; numb your throat and all that it touches. I prefer the sprays over the balms because with balms, you have to stick a finger down your throat in order for it to really be effective. With the spray, one squirt down your throat (not on the tongue), swallow after that and you are good to go. Beware, although this gets the job done, try to spray the throat and wait some minutes. If you immediately put your mouth on his penis (without a condom) it can numb him, too. Also, sometimes it will numb your entire mouth, also. But don't worry, that won't stop you from giving your man oral pleasure.

> There are also flavored condoms you can use. If you are allergic to latex, vinyl based (polyurethane) products can be used with a water/silicone based flavored product of your choice. Let us know what's the best tasting condom out there.
> www.VSGseries.com
> **If you want to use condoms for fear of tasting his penis versus protection... that's another issue itself.**

Household Goodies

Make him your Sunday Delight. Add some whip cream on top of his penis and around his buddies. Drizzle chocolate sauce everywhere, even on the stomach and top it off with a cherry for yourself. You should know what's the banana. Don't forget to suck the big delicious banana... just don't bite it! It's nothing wrong with having 2 cherries with your Sunday Delight - you eat the cherry off him, but save the best cherry for him... *YOURS*.

As I stated earlier, think of your favorite desserts when you go down on him. Word of caution, don't use anything spicy on his

The Sticky Ickey of Things

penis, it could feel like it's burning him. If you are going to make love after the oral act, make sure he's completely cleaned off before he enters inside you. If not, this could cause you to get a yeast infection.

The Goal is Simple

Use whatever you need to make it fun and tasty for the both of you. Making the oral experience good for you will make you do it more often.

Products you can use to make his cume taste better: Look for the V.S.G. and E & M Co line of tasty products and other seductive treats

Have you booked your party today?
We wanna be on TV, Documentaries, The Radio and at Seminars sharing this information with others
SPREAD THE WORD
We need your help and your business

Class is in Session
What color are You?

Get Ready... Get Set...
Go Go Gadget
Mind, Hands & Mouth

Chapter 7

The Gray Area and Creating a NEW YOU

with

Positions, Tips & Techniques for every occasion

Creating a NEW YOU

What the mind thinks, the body does

If you ever saw the cartoon *Inspector Gadget,* you know you have to remain flexible with all types of tricks up your sleeves and make sure you are butt naked under that rain coat. You've got to have one hand doing this... while the other hand is doing that... as your lips are moving like this... as you are seductively acting like that... don't forget to suck like this... and make sure you moan like that... don't forget to look like this... Oh! Don't forget to brace yourself for that... while you balance your body like this... DAMN! Your head might be spinning right now. Yep! All this work with no pay! Just remember, if your man is good at his oral craft, he's acting like Inspector Gadget, on you, with no pay, too.

The first thing that stimulates your man's penis is your mind. What keeps him erect and wanting more is the touch and stroke of your hands. What turns him on and finishes the climatic act is your mouth and your technique. What will make this all worth it for you is the comfort zone you've create for yourself. You should always redevelop your oral craft and deprogram yourself with the man you really care about and one that cares about you, also. This is the start of foreplay for him and how comfortable you become at satisfying him. You're in control at that very moment because you are initiating the acts to come. Rubbing on your man's penis is foreplay for

Class is in Session
What color are You?

you, also. When he's hard, you know what's about to come, and your body responds to what your hands feel. Your nipples harden along with the heavy breathing, and you are ready because he's ready. So in actuality, you are excited because you feel his excitement. But when you don't feel an erection, you feel something isn't right, that affects your arousal, in return, this affects the mood. Foreplay isn't stimulating anyone and the both of you really don't know what to do after that. So, as I stated earlier, if your mind isn't in it - his body won't respond to you. It's not that he's not in to you or he's a cheat; a brotha can sense when you don't want to perform oral sex. That makes him feel you don't want him! Yes! This is true.

Your hands (not hand) are essential in the oral act. A hand job should be an introduction to your mouth and what's to come. Hand jobs are good if the two of you are in a situation where Oral Sex really can't be done. Although excitement lies within the potential of getting caught, it is not sexy to get arrested for blowing your man off in public. Many of us do what we were taught, you stay in the black area - safety zone or predictability or you act reckless and venture into the white area.

Go Gray and DO DA DAMN THANG!!

Just talkin about the color of crayons - Not about people

Creating a NEW YOU

> **My Motto—Ride in the *Gray* Area:**
> It's sexy, fun, somewhat spontaneous and you won't fall asleep due to boredom, nor will someone have to pay your bail to release you from jail.

The *Black* Area is so predictable and confined: *In the Black area,* you are waiting in a long line for movie tickets, he strokes your face and run his finger across your mouth and you say, *"Stop It!" "Don't do that, everyone can see us!"* He just had a flash back of being at the show with his mother, when he was younger. Now, he's holding your hand like a controlled child.

The both of you go into the theatre, eat your popcorn and watch the movie you went to initially see. Finally, the movie ends, you get in the car, call to make sure the kids are ok. As you pick the kids up, you talk about how you enjoyed the movie and plan for the next night out with your man as the both of you go home. If any type of sex, especially Oral Sex, happens when you get home, get ready for lock jaw and tired hands. Good Luck at him doin *that* again! *BORING!* Foreplay should've started before you left the house, while you waited for the movie to start, during the movie and even during the drive home. Foreplay throughout the evening would have kept you both anxious to rock each other's world when you got home.

Chapter 7   **The Gray Area**

Class is in Session
What color are You?

The *White* Area is wild and extreme: *In the White area* - you got your **Hoe Gear** on with the boots to match. You are waiting in the long line to see the newly released Shrek III. Everyone is looking at the two of you because you both are lip locking in the line and oooozing the aura that you want to *fuck* right here — right now. As he pulls your hair, you moan in pleasure. His fingers runs across your lips. You stop his finger in front of your mouth; you began to lick and suck his middle finger as it goes in and out of your mouth over and over again. You stare into his eyes while the rest of the people are gasping and staring at the both you, in shock. He chases you into the theatre, and slaps your ass, you say *"OOOh! Big Daddy! That feels sooooo good!"* You sit in the middle row—the popular row and everyone can see *everything*,

While watching Shrek III, your man is rubbing your inner thigh as you raise your already short mini dress up to give him complete access to your goodies. You are noticeably squirming in your seat, then you start rubbing between his legs. You are definitely stroking his penis, as he has obviously risen to the occasion. The both of you are ready to get busy in the movie theatre and you're the center of attention because nothing is covering the both of you. Not to mention, the movie hasn't even started! People start complaining and shortly thereafter, the both of you are asked to leave the movie theatre.

Creating a NEW YOU

It's pretty obvious who is going to get sucked and fucked in the crowded movie parking lot. It's also NOT apparent that many theatres have hidden cameras watching the parking lot. They Do! Guess whose going to jail? Which child of yours will have to ask your mother to pick you both up from jail because you were caught performing lewd acts in the parking lot!? *OH! Guess who won't cume that night*!?

The *Gray* area is just right: *In the Gray area, you are strategic and creative.* The Gray area leaves unforgettable moments that will have him biting the palm of his hand every time he thinks of you and everything associated with that night you were standing in line to go see a *not* so popular movie. You're looking sexy in your mini dress, high heel boots and crotchless stockings with a sexy thong on underneath. Only your man knows what you have on underneath the long classy coat that ties in the front. You told him what you were wearing as you hugged and gently fondled him before the two of you got in the car to go to the movie. During the car ride to the movie, you say how sexy he looks and you are so turned on by it that you might have to get a *taste* of him when you get home. While he's driving, you're rubbing on his inner thigh, massaging his hard penis through his pants. At this point, he wants to go back home to continue the seduction. You tell him, *"No, baby let's have fun while we are together, without the kids."* As you wait in line for movie

Chapter 7   **The Gray Area**

Class is in Session
What color are You?

tickets, you stand in front of him, grabbing his arms, as he hugs you from behind. Afterwards, you look behind and up directly into his sexy eyes. Your lips are puckered up to insinuate you want a lil kiss. When he takes you up on your offer, you give him two pecks; one with a lil bit of tongue and the last peck lasts longer than 3 seconds. The ones in back can't see you. Most people are looking forward, following the flow of the line, so you stay blended in with the crowd. One side of his head blocks one side of the crowd, just leaving a possible glimpse from the other side. This is still arousing to the both of you, but not over the top in public. He strokes your hair – you smile. His hands touches your lips – you hold it there. You place your hand on top of his, and give moist gentle kisses on the inside of his hand. No one can see because you are both facing forward and your opened hands are covering the act. You both get a lil hot from it.

You enter the movie, holding each other's hand. Purposely. you look for a movie that's not crowded and sit in the highest row. Your man looks around, puzzled. You lick your lips, look at him and precede to slowly take your coat off–and say *"Do you like my outfit?"* As he excitedly responds *"YES!"* you sit down and place your coat over each other's lap. Underneath the coat, you guide his hand between your thighs, making sure he can explore your crotch-less stockings. You are secretly touching, massaging and fondling

Creating a NEW YOU

each other through the entire show. This keeps the foreplay going while you anticipate going home. After the movie is over, you're holding hands, going to the car talking about how much you enjoyed the brief time spent alone together and committed to one another that this will happen more often. No one is talking about the movie or the kids; that's not what the night was about.

You are both ready to go home - you rock each other's world and pick up the kids in the morning and return the favor to the babysitter the following week. In the Gray area, seductiveness is the initiator of everything. The *Gray* area ends boredom and jail time. ***That's priceless*!**

Hands are the first impression

First rule of thumb, you want to be as comfortable as possible and be able to use both hands as much as possible when it comes to oral sex and sex too, for that matter. If you find yourself having to do a balancing act on your knees and toes that requires the use of one of your hands also; you are probably not comfortable and you will become easily tired, frustrated and you'll use that as a reason to stop. If anything is uncomfortable, you won't do it, no matter how much you promised. It will show on your face, in your technique, and he can tell you don't want to and he'll have the impression that it's something wrong with him.

When it comes to the initial stage of foreplay, rubbing his penis with his pants on can be very arousing for the both of you. You can also use your leg to rub against his penis. You have to know when to unbuckle his pants and continue to stroke him through his underwear. The myth is you can have any type of clothes on during foreplay. Certain materials rubbing against the skin are a super turn on and can lead to him cumming, in his clothes. Awkward, especially if he has to leave after the wetness. Materials such as: latex, silks, smooth polyesters and other materials that easily slide over the body can keep your man aroused longer and keep the body anticipating more. This is also an added pleasure for you because you can see and feel how he respond to the things you are doing to him. If you enjoy grinding (performing sexual positions with clothes on and no penetration), you can cume from those materials rubbing against your body, also. If you *rub on top of his underwear,* while he is in the height of his arousal, this can decrease the amount of time you will give oral.

Now you are ready to take the pants and underwear off and get started with a brief hand job. Don't forget to have your lube of choice on hand. They do make purse-size lubes. When performing any type of sex act, you want to concentrate on the extremely sensitive parts of his penis (the foreskin, coronal ridge, frenulum and the testicles) to produce and maintain his erection. You must work the entire shaft during foreplay.

Toe Curling Tips and Techniques

While giving a hand job, remember you can't be too light handed. Men are more sensitive to unlubricated hands, scraping nails, ruff skin and teeth. Just the right pressure awakens all his senses. How good you are at your hand job is determined by the pressure you use. To give you an idea of how much pressure to use – take your writing hand and grab your forearm (about 2 inches from your wrist) with your thumb, index and middle finger. Try to touch your fingers with your thumb. You might not be able to form a circle, but you can feel when it becomes too tight and uncomfortable. That's the starting pressure to use on your man - I remind you again, don't forget your *sticky ickey* of choice - lube, saliva, etc. Always ask your man how it feels when you do this or that. Let him walk you through how much pressure to use where and when. If you are still unsure, it's simple; Just ask your man! He will tell you! Just don't ask him every 2 seconds, *"how does this feel."* That can become very annoying and will prolong your hand job and piss him off.

> ### ***Rule of thumb***
> Perform *whatever hand/finger position* around your forearm first (with a lube). Start about 2-3 inches from your wrist, the area where the arm gets wider and has more adipose (fatty) tissue. Squeeze gently until you can see a slight indentation on your skin and you can feel pressure from your entire hand around the forearm. Start off with that kind of pressure around the sensitive part of his penis; look at/feel how his penis reacts to what you are doing.
> If he is steadily getting harder or stays firm...
> keep doin what you're doin.

Chapter 7   **Positions for Every Situation**

Essential Hand Positions

Roll of the Dice
This requires all fingers and your palm

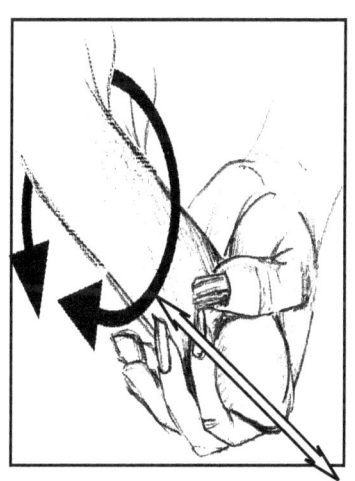

There are a couple of finger and hand positions that are essential in making foreplay, in regards to Oral Sex, pleasurable for both of you.

You want to use your strongest hand (your writing hand) by the head of the penis; especially around the coronal ridge and frenulum. The pressure from the hand below your strongest hand represents warmth and the tightness similar to him being inside the vagina. Gently massage the penis with a lubricant. Glide fingers and palm, lightly up and down and in circular, rhythmic movements that extend beyond the head, concentrating around the coronal ridge to about 2 inches on the shaft. This is the key to his pleasure and will decrease your hand fatigue. **_DO NOT_** change hands at the peak of his arousal. Just follow his lead in regards to how fast he moves. His enjoyment comes from the consistent pressure in a rhythmic movements you produce. This is why it is essential for you to be in a comfortable position and to also use your mouth for that moist warm feeling he needs to stay at a heightened arousal.

The OK Finger Position

Requires just the thumb,
the middle and index finger

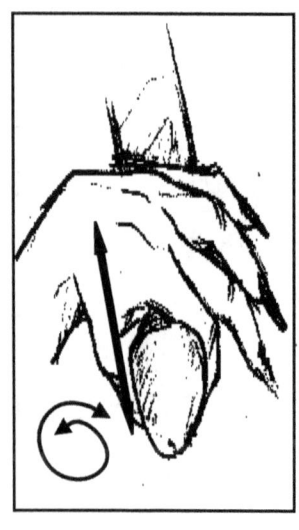

This position can cover about 2 to 3 inches of the shaft up to the very tip of the urinary opening (the pee hole). The gentle turning of the wrist and hands, versus straight up and down, will stimulate the sensory nerves from all angles. Make sure your thumb is rubbing against the frenulum as much as possible. Your other hand can stimulate the testicles simultaneously or can keep the skin nice and firmly held down at the base of the shaft. Use a lubricant as you stroke and twist his penis. This will intensify his pleasures 100 percent.

The Vertical Rub

Up and Down with the thumb
& tongue on the Frenulum   This is an ideal movement when you want to concentrate on one of the most sensitive areas of the penis. This also gives your entire hand a break. You want to finalize the hand job/oral act with the *roll of the dice* position combined with certain mouth movements in order for him to cume. Many ladies use the **OK** **position** at the wrong time. This is best used in the beginning when he is hard to the middle of the act.

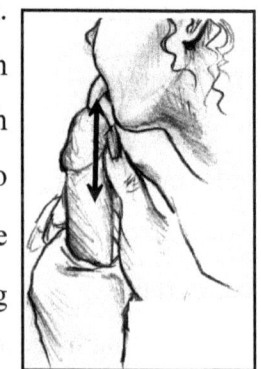

The Weapon

Now, up to this point, you should realize your state of mind is the most powerful thing you have. Your hands help bring what you are thinking to light, and this will send him through the roof. But your *ultimate* physical weapon, ounce for ounce, is your mighty tongue. The tongue - of course you know is the bottom muscle of the mouth; by size comparison, it is one of the strongest and hardest working muscle of your body. To my knowledge, it is one of 2 muscles that can start a war, cause permanent emotional harm and can motivate a person or a nation to move mountains. The other muscle I will talk about in detail in the next book.

Oooh! Your powerful tongue can cause a brotha to get soft like playdo or hard enough to break bricks. It all depends on what you say *before*, *during* and *after* the oral act. And, most importantly, how you use your tongue *while* giving head will set you apart from the alright group and catapult you to an *Oral Diva* and make a brotha shiver with delight every time he thinks about you.

Toe Curling Tips and Techniques

The POSSIBLE icing on your man's Oral Experience
Tongue Rings and other Oral Gadgets

Tongue piercing is becoming more popular because now many people think they're cute. It adds a shock value when you talk, and you can't convince me otherwise that some sistas purposely get their tongue pierced because they enjoy the sexual stares from brothas you can see foaming at the mouth over all the things they *think* that person can do sexually with the tongue ring. Well, my hat goes off to the tongue-pierced sista. Although tongue piercing was initially for religious and cultural reasons centuries ago, now especially in the US, it does have a sexual undertone. That added pressure on and around the coronal ridge, the knowledge from this book, the added confidence you have from feeling sexier and the *thoughts* of your man and about what you can do to him, with your tongue ring can be the icing on his oral cake.

From moms to porn stars, everyone is sporting seductive piercings, and many (men included) boost about what they can do with their pierced tongue. Even when women see a brotha with piercings, especially the tongue, our minds go into sexual mood, also. No matter what you say, brothas look at you at that moment and form an opinion; and from there, you attract a variety of brothas (some women want you, too). Now, as I always say, you must do what works for you, but you make less mistakes choosing the right brotha when you don't have to wonder what hundreds of brothas and sistas are thinking about you with all the exposed piercings and tattoos.

Although I consider myself to be an Oral Diva, I have no permanent tattoos. And, the only piercing I sport are the ear piercings I received as an infant. I don't want the looks or the imagination of what brothas think I can do. Their thoughts are probably right, but my skillz are just for my man, THAT'S JUST ME! No offense!

Now, back to the piercings. You can make oral sex more pleasurable for your man with a tongue ring, but it doesn't have to be permanent. There are all types of vibrating gadgets that can go around your tongue and/or his penis, that will boost your oral skillz. If you have your tongue pierced, there's also vibrating rings and rings with various textures that can be used to enhance your oral skillz.

Unfortunately, an even larger majority of these sistas sport the piercings and strategically placed sexual tattoos to get noticed and – *Now What*–Still No *Sucky Sucky*, and to top it off, some women will curse a man out if he comments on what he sees.

Didn't you do it for the attention?

> **Check where your tongue is pierced!** Usually if you are into women, the piercing is closer to the front. If you are into men, it sits further back on your tongue. *You know why*!
> **Check your man's pierced tongue... It can say a lot!**

Toe Curling Tips and Techniques

Your man's penis is equivalent to a large lollipop. Sucking on a lollipop with just your mouth alone is nowhere near as effective or tasty as using your mouth, lips and tongue simultaneously.

> **Big Fact** - many women are too gentle when it comes to touching and sucking the penis. Although the penis is sensitive, it's only a small area that is extremely sensitive and a lot of *controlled* lubricated friction is needed for it to feel good to him.

A quick experiment - place your finger in your mouth and just use your lips to suck. Now, all at the same time, use your mouth and tongue to suck, glide and lick over your finger. Try to remove your finger from your mouth while sucking on it. This should be hard to do. You will see you have a lot more precise sucking control. The goal is when your mouth is over his penis (majority of the shaft), you want to minimize the air that is in your mouth and form a suction on his penis, similar to when you tried to take your finger out of your mouth. When you use your sucking action with your tongue combined, this is the perfect time to concentrate on the sensitive areas of the penis (frenulum and coronal ridge). You will also be able to breathe through your nose with no problem.

This oral sex thing might seem simple enough, but many sistas gag because of improper breathing techniques versus he's too big. Many women will get discouraged and stop if it doesn't feel right. I don't want you to have ANY reason not to!

Chapter 7   Positions for Every Situation

It is your priority to control the deep throat action. More times than not, your man thrusts harder or grabs your head so the both of you move to the rhythm he needs to cume. It's hard for your man to tell you what to do at that point when he's in that euphoric high. You start to gag because you're resisting his rhythm. Now, you start to feel restricted and not in control. Your breathing becomes altered as you gag even more. He's still trying to grab your head/hair and continues to thrust. This throws him off and angers you, and you both are back at square one.

Welcome to my life and other sistas... once upon a time

That's all it took to discourage me from giving head back in the day. Now, I know why my man did what he did, and I share this with you because that is one of the reasons why I felt that oral sex was degrading. The lack of control scared me, too. The new and improved me anticipates his rhythm change, his penis pulsations, butt tightening and toe spasming movements.

It's no surprise anymore - I Is Ready NOW!

> I can't count the times I've held my man's face down on my precious jewel (clitoris) without feeling guilty about exploding in his mouth or the slight suffocation he might be going thru. He's turned on knowing he has satisfied his baby and eagerly awaits for me to return the favor.

Toe Curling Tips and Techniques

Neck – Lean Back
Your Nose Knows

Just like any other lovemaking session, you really can feel when his explosion is about to come. You brace yourself, moan and smile, then hold on tightly. Fatigue and oral sex can go hand in hand if your form is not correct. How your head is held and how your neck is positioned will determine how much of your man you can really take in without gagging. If your head is facing forward or slightly downward while performing oral sex, gravity will naturally add weight to your tonsils, thus making it harder for you to be able to breathe through your mouth. These head positions are not bad; you just need to know what positions are comfortable for you * what position will produce what effect * what do you want the outcome to be (him to cume or help with his erection) * and what do you want to happen between the two of you afterwards?

Your nose is apart of your sensory organs and can magnify your taste buds. Don't purposely sniff around your man's body parts looking for bad odors... *You know you will find some* :?

When you truly deep throat, you should be holding your breath, but not as if you are under water. Instead, relax your throat, elevate your neck upward. Don't go so far back that it affects how you breathe. Your lungs should be comfortably filled with air.

Chapter 7   **Positions for Every Situation**

> **Remember**, deep throating is more of a visual and because of that, it can be an added tool in helping him cume. You don't have to deep throat for hours and face tonsil replacement when you know the true reason for deep throating.

Once you've mastered your breathing, you can make him cume quicker and minimize your suffering from hand, neck and mouth fatigue.

Cliff Notes of what you just read

Breathe through your nose and use your, lips, mouth and tongue simultaneously for maximum suction, especially when you want to focus on a specific area of his penis.

To prevent gagging when deep throating, relax your throat muscle. When he starts to thrust quickly, just follow his rhythm, and start to deep throat. Gain control of his movements and calmly hold your breathe. Saliva should be over-following by now. Extend your neck for comfort. Everything that you have in your oral arsenal should be utilized when you want to master your oral sex skillz - your mind, hands, mouth, tongue, lubes, body position, sound effects, sight, eagerness to please and confidence will keep you holden IT down as the Diva in your man's world.

You might be thinking *Damn... That's a Lot of Work!* It really isn't. It only takes 2-5 minutes for a Diva to make a brotha's toes curl.

Toe Curling Tips and Techniques

Last BUT Definitely Not Least

Before you use any hand, mouth or position - YOU MUST know your man's anatomy. How they hang (penis and balls), which testicle is the most sensitive to touch and which testicle can be licked and/or sucked to help him reach cloud nine. What's the curvature of his penis? The majority of men don't hang straight down. What ever you do, try to keep it all in the natural state they rest in. You will achieve the best results and response from him. Of course, some brothas enjoy it the opposite way... OUCH! Simply ask him what he likes, beforehand, he knows his body better than you.

Lets Put It All Together

How you put all that you have read together is what makes the difference between your techniques and mine.

Is it time for your
Ladies Nite Hen Party
Call (708) 868-4122
for a rep in your area

Also visit
www.villagesistagirlfriend.com
To find vibrating tongue gadgets
And
Permanent and Non Permanent
body jewelry and tattoos

Chapter 7   Positions for Every Situation

Thumb up, a Knuckle, a Cup Position And TWO Snaps

Requires both hands for maximum coverage and the knuckle to stimulate the perineum

NOT *'Two Girls and a Cup'....*

That was just disgusting!

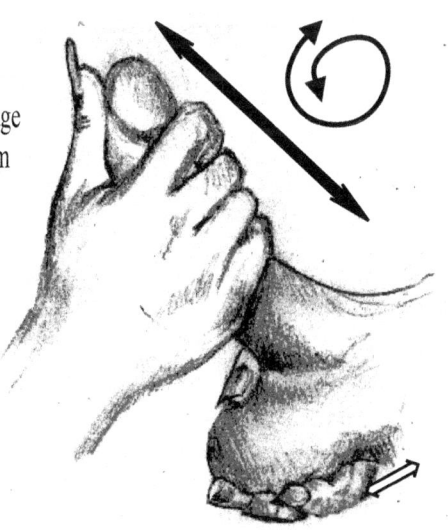

Don't forget to extend the knuckle to stimulate the perineum

With this position, you have your strongest hand around the top portion of his penis, adding extra - pressure around the coronal ridge, while your thumb is in an upward position applying separate pressure to the frenulum. Your tongue and mouth reinforces the heat, pressure and slidability of your fingers. The other fingers act like the vagina, supplying heat and light friction to the shaft. You are also able to cup the testicles for support and apply light rhythmic movements, while your index knuckle is slightly raised, stimulating the perineum. This hand position allows you to work and cover the entire shaft. The entire penis, the testicles and the perineum are massaged, at the same time, without overworking your hands. Remember, you must have both hands lubed with a silicone or water-based product to prevent dryness.

To Master this position you are using everything you know

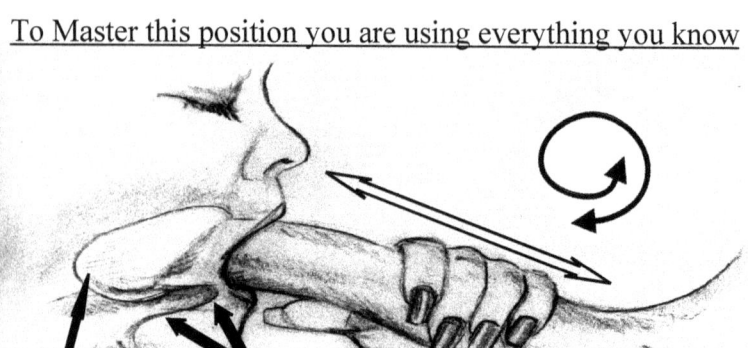

Use jaw muscle for maximum suction

glide w/ your tongue

> **Note: For maximum pleasure**
> Even inside the mouth, use your tongue to glide back & forth over the frenulum. Good breathing techniques will ease the throat muscles & minimize gagging. Use your jaws for ultimate control. You must cup and massage the testicles at the same time. Nicely firm lips concentrating on the coronal ridge with your mouth overflowing with saliva and lube will make him cume quickly. OOH! Don't forget your sounds, gauge at his responses...
> **All this is done at the *SAME* TIME**

This is a perfect way for you to perform oral sex on him. Not only will he be able to hear your moans, but this is a comfortable for you, too. Especially, if you are sitting down. He will also get a lot of eye candy as he watches what you do to him in your sexy lingerie & heels, your business suit or your sexy club wear you use to wear to get his attention. AND, when you've mastered the craft of not fainting when you taste his cume... *WHALA*... You've got it! After his toes stop curling and his body spasms stop, give yourself...

Chapter 7   Positions for Every Situation

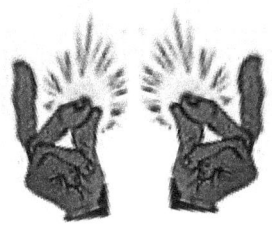 ## Two Snaps! You GOT This!!!!

This is a great technique for a sista who has mastered the rhythmic motions of her man, knows how to follow his lead, has asked for and listened to all the things he said he likes when it comes to pleasing him orally and has conquered the fear of completing the oral act (*swallowing*). If you are thinking why swallow if this hand technique can send him through the roof by itself - that's a great question! I can answer it like this! Although cake can taste good by itself, most prefer sweet icing to be on top of it. Swallowing is your man's icing on his cake.

Sit Down:

This is a great position for both of you. The **Benefit to you:** (the giver) is less work and no sore jaws. You want to be in a position where you have both hands available to massage, stroke, and cup your man's penis and testicles.

Toe Curling Tips and Techniques

As you become more comfortable with the act and your skills improve, it is your ultimate mission to be able to massage, stroke, suck, cup, moan, and a couple of other things I will mention later... *ALL* at the same time. You should already know, you must be a multi-tasker in order to be a successful Blow Jobber.

The *Sit Down* **position**, allows you to be in a position where you are using muscles you *normally* use. You don't have to be a porn star and be uncomfortable. The goal is to satisfy him and prevent muscle spasms for you. When you are comfortable, your stroke is less jerky and it's less likely you will stop in the middle of the act from cramps and spasms. Your man can move as quickly or slowly as he likes without you gagging, *IF* you move with his rhythm **And** use at least one of your hands (preferably your strongest hand - the one you write with) in front of your lips, (stimulating the coronal ridge and the frenulum) so it feels like his entire penis is blanketed by the inside of your warm wet mouth, he can get harder a lot faster and be ready to go inside you. The other hand should be used to cup the balls and massage the perineum. If you lose your rhythm or you and he lose sync with each other, just place your hand on his waist, buttocks, or stomach for control again. This is a major turn on for him when it *appears* that either you are taking control or he is so huge that you can *barely* take in all of him. **Yeah Right!**

Chapter 7 Positions for Every Situation

> **Meaning: No matter how good you feel you are at the act of Oral Sex, it feels better if there's no restrictions.
> You can't be at your best with restrictions.**

The Ultimate Position
For maximum comfort and minimization of fatigue

You must have the willingness to practice and **practice** mastering your techniques while you have the lights on. High heels and other eye candy are a definite plus, but your man hearing your moans and seeing your slurps of pleasure and sounds of his favorite porn star while glancing at his favorite DVD, in the background, will send him through the roof, and you too, if you let it.

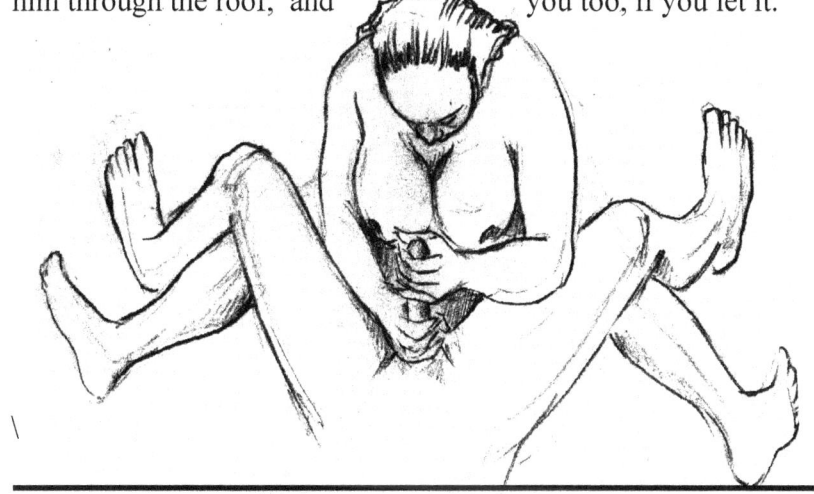

Toe Curling Tips and Techniques

When you are completely comfortable and your skillz are tight, you can have uncombed hair, no makeup, a cast on your leg and crust in your eyes—**You Will Still Send** a brotha through the Roof with his toes curled, eyes rolled back and a smile on his face.

__The Everything and More Pretzel #1__
For the advance suckers

There are so many ways you can turn this position into an oral masterpiece. That's why it's called *the Everything and More Pretzel*. His knees can be elevated by pillows so he can comfortably thrust backwards toward your mouth. Your body can be elevated higher so you can thrust in a downward motion to minimize neck fatigue and gagging. If he has a large stomach, back problems or if he's truly 12 inches, you control how much you take in.

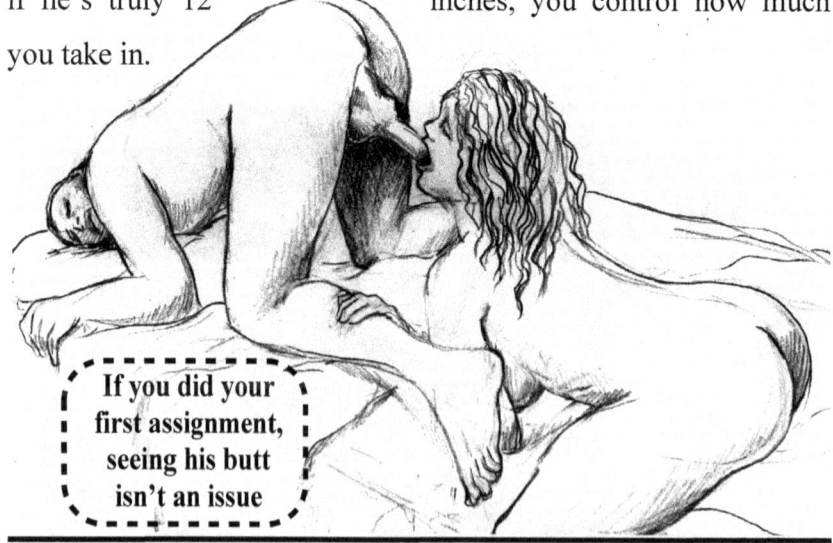

> If you did your first assignment, seeing his butt isn't an issue

The Everything and More Pretzel #2
Another variation

In the *Everything and More Pretzel,* you can lay on your back as he straddles your face. Your neck is supported by pillows, of course. His hands are free to stimulate your nipples or massage your clitoris with his fingers or use an orgasmic *viiiibraaating* toy! The both of you are comfortable and able to thrust to each other's rhythm. And he's moving the most—this can intensify his oral experience.

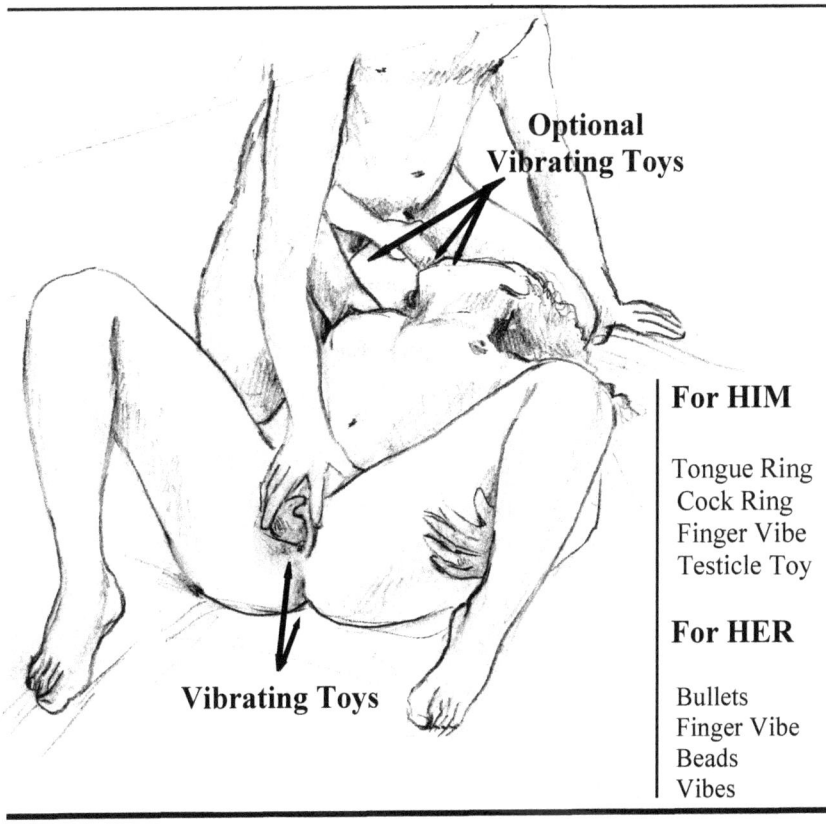

Optional Vibrating Toys

Vibrating Toys

For HIM

Tongue Ring
Cock Ring
Finger Vibe
Testicle Toy

For HER

Bullets
Finger Vibe
Beads
Vibes

Toe Curling Tips and Techniques

The Traditional 69
oral sex performed on each other simultaneously

Usually that's when you're horizontally on the bed, the woman is on top of her man, facing his feet and performs oral sex on him. At the same time, the man is on the bottom, while the woman is on all fours, her vagina is in his face ready to be eatin by her man.

I've picked up some pounds over the years and so has my huzband - *we still look good though,* but I feel like a stuck whale on a beach, and I am suffocating the both of us. This is why this is not a favorite of mine. But there are other ways to do the 69. Both can be on each other's side with legs open and knees bent. Expect one person to cume first when doing the 69 position (usually the female). When I am in an orgasmic bliss, I can't get in sync with him because my body is enjoying what he's doing too much. As a result, he will probably maintain his erection, but I will be exhausted afterwards but wanting to return the favor. That's why I prefer the *Alternative 69 - The 61 incentive.* Here, you are more in sync with each other without restricting the other's movement. There's no balancing act for either of you, so no one is tired. The added incentives are you can use toys, your fingers and gadget to stimulate every inch of your body, no stomachs are in the way, you can maintain separate rhythmic motions that will allow you both to orgasm closer together. If you need more stimulation, you can do it yourself AND

Stayed focused on watching your favorite XXX DVD... OMG-WTF!

Your ORAL Diva
www.villagesistagirlfriend.com

The Alternative to the 69
The 61 incentive

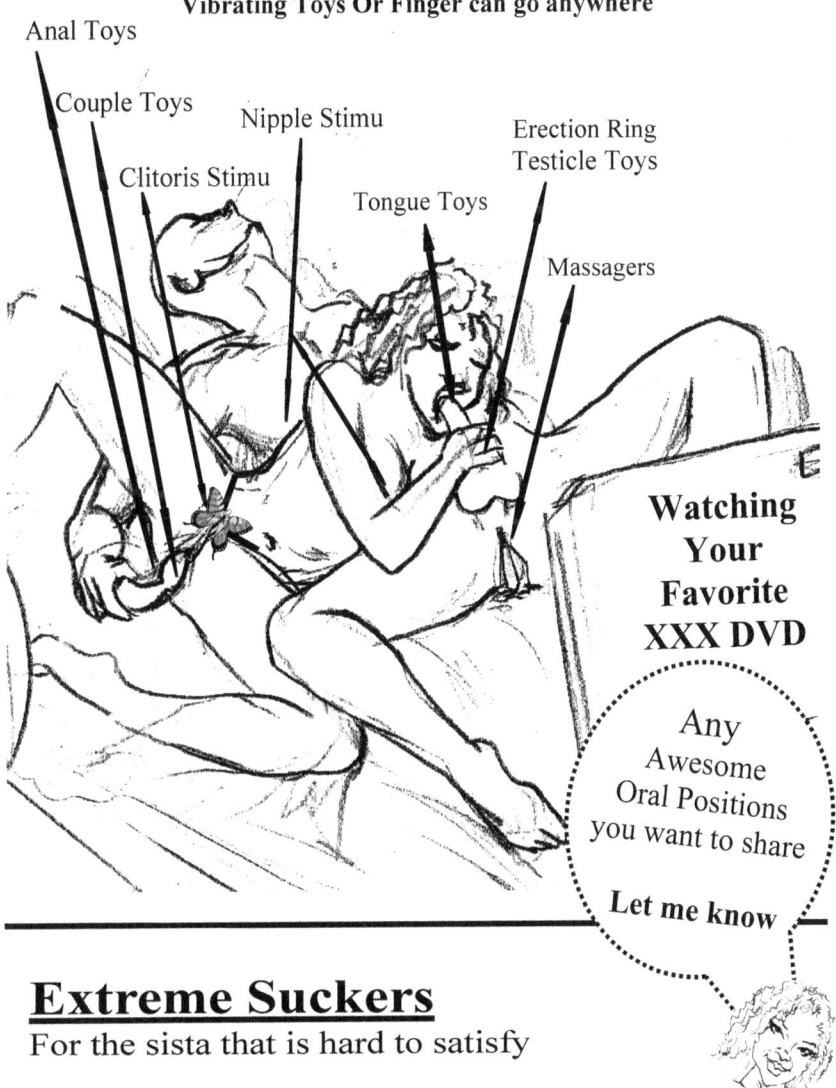

Extreme Suckers
For the sista that is hard to satisfy

Proceed with caution when going to the next page. The illustration is simple, but you must visualize what I am talkin about to get it.

Toe Curling Tips and Techniques

Over the years, I have met sistas that only wanted soft and gentle lovemaking. All that ruff stuff in the bedroom was a no-no. In my opinion that was boring - *All the Time.* Then I realized I too, belonged to a group. "Face Down - Ass Up" "Bend Over - Grab Your Ankles and Brace *Yo*self Fool" YES!... YES! I love an occasional G.F. (Gut Fucking) and hair pulling. I'm not alone. That means, I challenge myself to new plateaus when it comes to creating new love techniques with my huzband. I try to take it all in, work on my breathing and don't gag. But Damn! I have yet to master F.F. (Face Fucking). There are some DVD's I've watched where I am convinced that they have had some type of throat surgery in order to be able to have a penis fully thrusting in and out of the mouth with such extreme force. These positions are for the sista that has went past the G.F. To fisting or just feel they can handle *ALL* of him at *any* thrusting speed. Your man can stand over you and thrust downward or place a pillow behind your head while kneeling against a wall. This is for maximum F.F. (Face Fucking)...

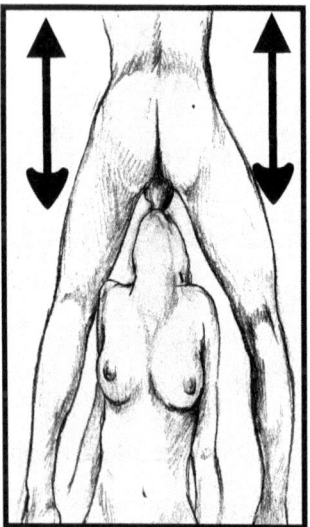

If that's your thing.

> **Caution**
> Must be at your (OTP)
> Oral Training Peek
> for this And have
> great Medical Insurance.

Chapter 7   **Positions for Every Situation**

" What's wrong with this picture?"

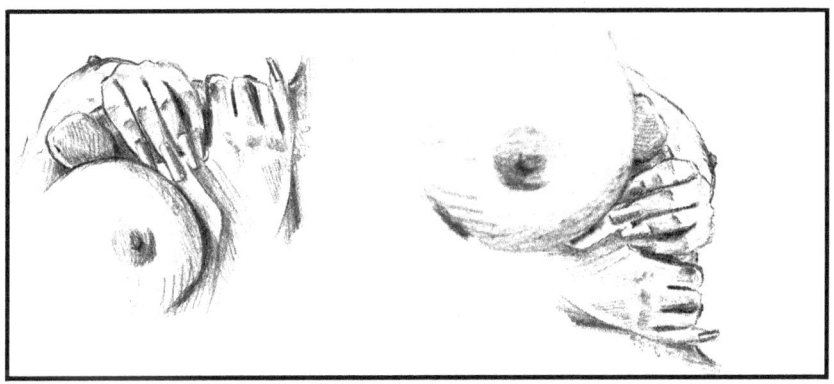

Contrary to what you might think; it's not about breast size. Breast only provides a visual picture for him. If your technique isn't there, don't waste your time with a breast appetizer. It's more about being confident, knowing the most sensitive parts of his penis and how to stimulate his mind. Most importantly, you're taking control of the situation with your words and sound effects - that will drive him through the roof.

Some of the most arousing positions can be with you on your knees. Some complain that it hurts their knees. **SIMPLE FIX**: Place a pillow or blanket under your knees. Men do not care if you are on your knees comfortably versus painfully kneeling down in front of

Toe Curling Tips and Techniques

him. What he wants from you is you comfortably giving head with no reason to stop.

Also, a lubricant is a plus between the breast. You still must utilize your mouth. Don't turn your head, but instead suck, lick and talk dirty to him. With the warmth and suction of your mouth and the soft tissue of your breast, it feels very close to the softness of your vagina.

Make sure you are caressing the coronal ridge with your hands and/or mouth as he moves up and down between your breast. The key to his enjoyment is your sucking action and the sound effects.

Chapter 7   **Positions for Every Situation**

Big FACT

Your man doesn't really want you to suck like a *porn star*. Instead, he wants you to be confident in yourself and what you do, *like* a porn star *portrays*. He wants to be the center of your sexual attention, like a porn movie is designed for him to envision himself in the act. He wants to be desired by his woman who doesn't mind, *Droppin Like It's Hot,* like when he sees a porn star that has no problem with switchin positions or moaning as she stares in to his eyes thorough the TV. Your man is not envisioning you sucking off 3 men at a time in slut gear.

That's Your Imagination Gone Wild

No different than us – we want a confident brotha who has no problem with doin whatever it takes to please us sexually. The only difference is our stimulating porn is in the erotic books we read, the lovemaking songs we sing and the girl flicks we watch.

Toe Curling Tips and Techniques

When it's all said and done, the Oral Sex positions in this book have many benefits for women:

- You are in control of how much you take in your mouth
- Both hands are available to stimulate him and/or yourself
- The magical part, he can stimulate you with his fingers, hands and/or toys
- You are both being turned on simultaneously
- He is able to watch what you are doing, as a result, he is aroused more with less work from you
- And an added plus - if you are somewhat uncomfortable with your body, you are in positions that help conceal some of the areas (the stomach, breast, and arms) we complain about.

As I have stated in the past, your man is not looking at you with a criticizing eye. When he is on cloud nine, his eyes are in the back of his head. The more comfortable and turned on the both of you are, the better the experience will be for the both of you.

Chapter 7   **Positions for Every Situation**

A Selfish Oral Sexless Sista's Dream

Meeting a man who says he's not into getting head - and he's not a religious fanatic

If a brother tells you he doesn't want head, proceed with caution!

Men love receiving head! That's a fact! Although men want oral, there are a few men that have a double standard that is senseless and dangerous.

"I don't want my wife kissing my kids with that mouth!"
Some women that don't want to go down on their man think he's the perfect gem. That same brotha that doesn't want head from you, his woman, sometimes require head from the other woman *"that will"* - that's his *"Mistress"* requirement. I am not saying every brotha will do this that doesn't want his woman giving him head, but don't think he's gold because he told you he didn't want it from you!

> If you are the brotha that disagrees with this statement, feel free to voice your opinion. As long as you are not a religious fanatic, had a bad experience with oral or has a small penis and you are self conscious - please email the reason(s) why you don't like to have oral sex performed on you by your wife or the woman you love.
> www.VSGseries.com
> and Face Book or join the forums and/or blogs

Toe Curling Tips and Techniques

www.VSGseries.com
Change Starts with YOU... Right NOW!

What Toys are you interested in? Call/Email and we can help

Save the original... MAKE COPIES

learn even more at your party
www.VSGseries.com

Assignment/Homework

Oral Sex & Toys used for the man with ED
(Erectile Dysfunction)

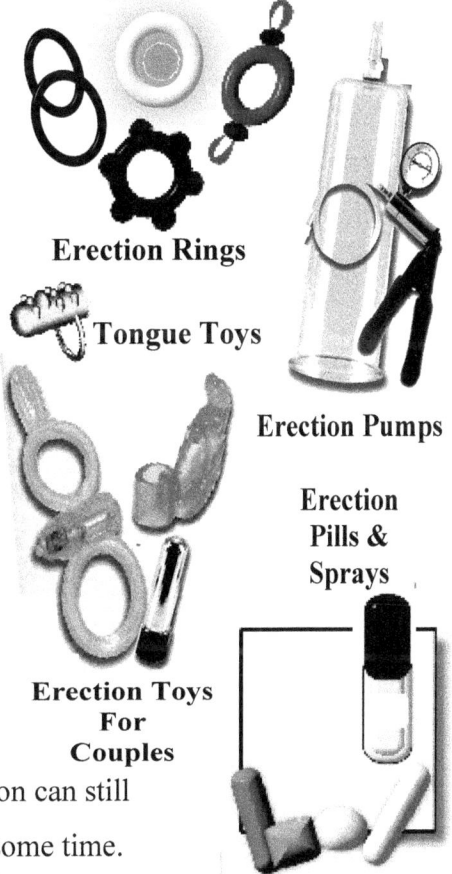

Erection Rings

Tongue Toys

Erection Pumps

Erection Pills & Sprays

Erection Toys For Couples

If you have read anything about men and aging, you might have read that a man's erections can become less firm as he gets older. That is true, but what you don't hear is, if your man has no major illness, vascular disease, life style changes, or side effects from medications, his erection can still remain very firm, for quite some time.

> **Some of the reasons that can cause ED**
> - Health Conditions
> - Vascular Disease
> - Physiological
> - Relationship Issues
> - Insecurities
> - Medication
> - YOU
>
> (go online to find more info)

What many sistas don't know is ED effects millions of men (last checked over fifteen million) of all ages. So before you say, "He can't get it up... there's something wrong with *HIM*!", realize your man's erection starts mentally first. And just like you, he

Toe Curling Tips and Techniques

needs less stress from daily chores, children and more kissing and fondling from you to get him erect. You get it started and tell him what you want and he will do the same. ***What is foreplay for men of any ages?*** YEP! Oral Sex and REALISTIC Ego Stroking! Not lingerie stuff, like you are programmed to think. What you both need from each other is free.

Now, ED can also be a result of physical dilemmas that are apparent or not visible to you and your man. Every man will experience ED In their lifetime and on more than one occasion; but if 40% of the time the both of you are aroused, but he can't get an erection, you definitely should have him seek medical help. And even after medication is given to help with any ailments he might have; don't think all is well. It will be to your advantage to perform Oral Sex more often and also use toys and ointments that will help him maintain his erection.

That is why some women don't feel the importance of giving head. They don't know or care what the ED is caused by, as long as they don't have to give oral sex - it's all good, until the sex life suffers.

If you are fortunate enough to have a man that can still stay hard as a rock, he is less likely to be able to go all night in those *pretzel* like positions. Oral Sex becomes even more important for the both of you because with age should come a better quality of lovemak-

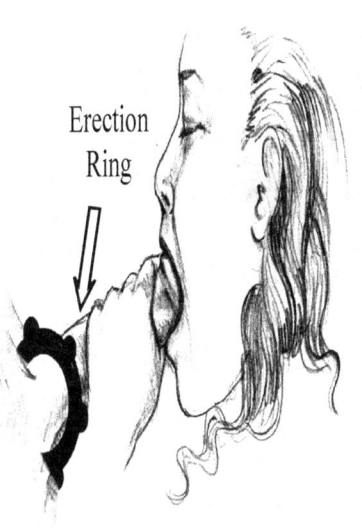

ing with an *occasional* gut pounding, leg cramping, breaking down the bed, hair pulling, and back scratching – got to call off work *episode*.

> **If you are eager to say *it must be him* instead of saying "what can _we_ do or how can _we_ make this work", you can also be the erection killer.**

When you were younger, what made you drip with sweat and breathe harder than an Olympic runner can now cause you to soak in a tub full of alcohol and Epson salt. Being known for popping pain pills and wearing the fragrance of Ben-Gay-

Is So Not SEXY!

Toe Curling Tips and Techniques

It doesn't take a rocket scientist to figure out your bodies can't handle back breaking sex, all the time. And why should you! Your lovemaking can be just as explosive without all the aches and pains. That is another priceless benefit to Oral Sex. It doesn't take hours to cume. If you know each other's bodies and what it takes to please each other, it literally can take less than fifteen minutes, for the *both* of you, to experience powerful orgasms. I am not saying you can't have good sex without oral but anyone that has had great Oral Sex, never wants to go back to an oralless relationship.

Some women feel that they cannot do anything to make a difference in the quantity or quality of their man's erections. That's so not true! If his erection dilemma is due to age and time, you can do more for him by offering more oral stimulation. Now, if he has a medical condition such as heart disease or diabetes and he doesn't take medicine for it, this could be something to be concerned about. He needs more than oral sex to overcome some problems. Sometimes pills, pumps and other medical items might be needed. Consult your physician.

No matter how much you say you love your man, high blood pressure, diabetes, vascular/heart disease or you continuing to be a selfish lover can sometimes make it impossible for your man to get and maintain an erection. These are silent killers that also can throw a curve in your sex life and destroy your relationship.

Chapter 7   Positions for Every Situation

Before you use the reason

"He must have one of those *conditions* - that's why *he can't get it up*," make sure you're not a part of the erection killers.

If he has an unknown condition combined with your negativity and you lack the willingness to try if it relates to oral, you are NOT part of the solution.

If you are eager to say it must be *him* instead of asking "what can *we* do", this will forever be a problem with any man you get involved with.

Toe Curling Tips and Techniques

Medical To Do List

List some of the symptoms you have noticed in your man.
Make an appt for a check up. Most women make the doctors appt. You can always talk to the Doctor about your concerns and ask for certain tests in relation to the symptoms you both might have noticed.

NOTE: Don't create symptoms - if you have to work on your oral skillz mentally- then it's simple! **Just Do IT!**

Appt with: _____ Appt when: _____

Your concerns _____

_____

_____

_____

_____

_____

_____

_____

How can *you* help the situation: _____

_____

_____

_____

_____

Assignment/Homework

Bring Out Your ORAL Diva
STEP OUT of YOUR BOX

Chapter 8

Puttin ALL You've Learned Together

Lights, Camera... ACTION!

Lights:

Men are visual. Your man needs to be able to see and feel you. I know many women (including myself) dislike their bodies when we are in one of our *blah* moods. No matter how beautiful our man tells us we are, we don't want to hear it. It's normal to feel this way because when your man tells you that, you can always go back in time when *you* really *felt* you *looked HOT*! As a result, many women (myself included sometimes) never feel good about ourselves physically in the present because we are (ppc) ***past picture chasers***. I guarantee, if you look at a picture of yourself when you were a couple of years younger, you will look at it now and say **"Damn I *Looked* Good!"** but you didn't feel that way the moment it was taken. So learn to say *Thank You Sweetie* (your pet name for your man) and practice appreciating your beauty.

Simple Solutions

Watch a XXX DVD - while you are performing oral sex on each other. This gives him visual and physical stimulation. All his senses are stimulated simultaneously and you look even greater under the glow of the TV. If you are uncomfortable with certain XXX DVD's, choose a DVD of *your* choice. Just make sure it's something that you will both like. That's the only fivesome that's safe -

Bring Out Your ORAL Diva
STEP OUT of YOUR BOX

toys for the both of you (2) + DVD's of choice (1) + and the two of you (2) = (fivesome) having fun and enjoying yourselves. When it comes to porn, there's something out there for everyone. Deprogram yourself, create your own XXX DVD collection. You can be more aroused when you have your favorites DVD to look at. Men and women look at porn differently, so your collection might be different than his. When selecting a porn DVD for the both of you, choose one that will turn you both on.

Lighting can be colored bulbs; black, blue, purple and red. There are even cooler colors out there. Lights are good to use to minimize things and set the mood. Neon signs and paintings gives off an awesome glow, too. The flashing fixtures that look like either a siren or traffic light are great and also very calming. Ask your man, you will find out that it doesn't have to be in broad daylight... he doesn't care. He just want to see it go into your mouth without you making him feel bad about looking at you.

Helpful Hint: Say to yourself – "I am sexy as hell! And I feel good!"

Solution: Create your own lighting. You don't have to do it in daylight with the sun bearing down on your head. As I said before, your man just wants to see you, not every single pore and hair follicle.

Lights, Camera... ACTION!

Camera:

Although you can't necessarily escape daylight, you can still be an *Oral Diva*. Do like the famous people – strike a pose and get in your best staged oral position. Example—If you don't want your stomach to show, get on your knees or lay on your back while he is facing you or standing over you. If your arms are not as toned as you would like them to be (join the club), simply sit on top of him, with your back towards his face. Although he doesn't see your head movements in this position, he can see your butt and silhouette while you simulate sexual acts and moans of pleasure (remember ego stroking). There are so many oral positions that make you look great. Just think of the parts of your body you don't want him to see and you can suck it in or position yourself accordingly.

Mirrors! OMG! Can be the sexiest thing ever. He can see everything and so can you. Large mirrors strategically placed in your favorite lovemaking spots, can give you that extra confidence boost. When it come to most brothas, they are turned on even more when they are in there *own* movie. Him being able to see you visually while giving head, turns him on mentally; plus the sounds being made... WOOOOOW! You can nail the mirrors on the ceiling with lights around. Just anchors everything to the studs and keep the mirrors lightweight - you've just created your getaway at home.

He can play with your vagina and clitoris with a toy or his fingers. In other positions, he's looking at your head movements and the techniques that are probably keeping his eyes slightly closed in an orgasmic bliss. He does not care about your imperfect body – no one is perfect... So enjoy yourself! If you stop the mental hangups, you will be turned by what you see too.

Action:

You already know the techniques, now you have to be creative and mix up all that you've learned. Customize your skillz for you and your man. Being able to use both hands, while you are in a comfortable position, as you utilize all the tips and techniques you've learned from the book, while performing oral sex, is priceless! Don't forget to smile and moan. *Action* depends on how you got it started. If you tell your man you've missed him over the phone and you can't wait to see him; you have put a good thought on his mind. That can lead to good *actions* being taken by the both of you. When giving head, you can do whatever you like, but the most effective way when starting out (my opinion) is when you take the role of the Exciter or the Submisser.

Lights, Camera... ACTION!

The Exciter

You're the moaner. When you say "OOH! Big Daddy!" or when you say "YES! BABY! I want more!" She has more of a feminine approach, with moans and facial expressions showing as if he's too big for her and he's just too much to handle. *Yeah Right*! You might be thinking. Just don't let him know that. This is a huge ego boost for him that will surely lead to him returning the favor. And, YOU WON'T BE DOWN THERE FOREVER.

Pros:

Awesome ego booster for him. When your man feels like you can't handle all of him, he actually becomes more excited. He doesn't see you as a threat or someone he just can't satisfy. When he feels like he is all that, he tends to go out of his way to be a better lover because he wants you to keep wanting him and he enjoys pleasing you.

Cons:

If he feels he's not doing it for you because you are not moaning enough or out of "complete actress mode," he will try to get you to sound like you are enjoy it. That can be tiresome and a lil painful for you.

Bring Out Your ORAL Diva
STEP OUT of YOUR BOX

The Submisser

When you ask "Can I?" - You are asking for permission and you are letting him control the situation. As the Submisser, you should ask "Do you like it like this, baby! (his pet name)" Basically, he's your Master/teacher and as his Slave/student, he tells you what to do.

Pros:

This makes him feel like he's in control; that can be a great thing because he tells you *how to* and *when to do* the things he needs to make him cume. He will explode in no time. You'll love the game.

You get to follow his lead. Less guess work for you, especially when you really are comfortable with performing oral sex on him now. You have learned his body from the assignments in the book and now you are ready to play the part. Also, you can be put in some crazy positions because he is in control exclusively. YEAH!

Cons:

This can make him lazy and forgetful of your needs. You have to remind and reiterate to him that you are learning to please him and not to forget you need pleasing, too.

Lights, Camera... ACTION!

The best Exciter and Submisser treats this like a dance; following his lead and knowing when to do what. Everyone looks and feels good when the leader leads and the follower follows. When in submissive mood, his visual is essential to his enjoyment. He wants to look at what you are doing. You don't have to look at him unless that's his request. Encourage him to talk where you can answer him in ways such as, "yes (his pet name)."

"Uh-huh (your pet name for him)" "like that (your pet name for him)." The Exciter will say something like, "I love to feel you in my mouth, "OHMYGOD!" "This is soooogoood!" Right now I know this sounds cheesy, but it's very effective in decreasing your oral sex time and fatigue.

I wanna hear you in exciter and submisser mood, visit us soon online or order the villagesistagirlfriend CD's. To find many of these items and supplies-go to www.VSGseries.com

Chapter 8   Lets GET IT Crackin

The Finale is

Overcoming your fears

Deprogramming yourself

Seeking Education

Motivating yourself and learning your man

Mastering your Oral Techniques

AND Not being afraid to show ALL your skillz to your man

AND JUST

Lights, Camera... ACTION!

188   Forums, Blogs and Specialist available online

Chapter 8   Lets GET IT Crackin

Step Out of Your Box

Chapter 9

Fears be gone

> Just like I decided to change from...
> daddy's good girl to the good wife -
> you can, too.
> What you do between
> you and your man to keep each other
> happy is your business.

Never Forget That

Step Out of Your Box

Let's Make a Movie

The *New You* has tips and techniques to make you an Oral Diva on a whole other level. The Comfy Coupons helped you overcome some of your concerns and your man should be excited that you are eager to please him. You learned about lighting and what you can do to make you look better when giving your man awesome head. You've learned so many ways you can give him oral sex and help you feel better about your body... that was in the camera segment. This entire book has prepared you for action. By now you have more confidence than what you had when you first opened the book and now you can **Step Out of Your Box** a lil more. Something so simple as creating a movie between the two of you has been viewed as hard or risky. Many people are paranoid about all that they do they will end up on TV or the video will be leaked out. My opinion - the videos that have been leaked to the press over the years was leaked by either the ones in the video or a close friend. I also think it was intentional. I say that, for this reason; that shouldn't stop you from having fun with your man. I am not talking about a *Dip* or *Friends with Benefits,* but your man that you trust and have already did some things that are making you blush as you think about it now. If you have a cell phone, it can be sexy to send seductive pictures to one another. Once again, to your man (huzband) not just to *erbody*. Check the laws in your state.

Chapter 9   **The Change**

Jail time is soooo Not Sexy and that's like so 40 seconds ago!! If it's more provocative then a pose, don't send a head shot. Only take a picture of the area(s) you want him to see. Include his information in your pic text. You can always give him a sample tease via pic text and say when you see him, he can get it all. This is the same for phones with video capabilities. You can go anywhere and send him a video. It can be you describing what you will do to him when you see him or what you want done to you. You can put sheer material over your phone as you record yourself doing what ever you want. Example - suck and play seductively with a candy bar as you tell your man what you will do to him when you see him. This is turning him on because he really can't see you because of the material. I don't know about you, but I am turned on when I am in control, sexually. It drives me wild knowing he's thinking about me in that way.

You and your man can make your own seductive movie starring - your chosen character names. My name - Wet Mouth Ace in the Hole (lol). **Get into Character.** Some times it's easier to be a lot more naughtier when you are acting as a character. Pick days and events when it's more common to either go out or dress up. Consider: Comic Conventions, Parades, Concerts, Halloween, Christmas Santa (I know, I'm sick), Forth of July just to name a few. There are all types of holidays, organizations and functions that require you

Step Out of Your Box

to get into character. Create a Date Night and get dressed up. Get ur hare did, wear a wig, put on your sexy heels, and stay in the *Gray Area.* You can make a movie at home or in a hotel. You don't need any special stuff. All you need these days are a cell phone that can record or a digital camcorder or a webcam and a computer for editing and adding sound effects. There's always free software available online and most of your desktop publisher software has movie editing features included. You will also need sheer see thru material and a lubricant of choice.

Go all out sometimes, get into character with costumes as simple as a basic mask and crotchless fishnets to as elaborate as feathers, gowns, furry animal costumes with the heads (lol). If you wear something over your face and cover up any distinctive marks on you, no one will know who you are except the two of you. If you wear facial costumes, no one will know who it is if it's ever discovered. What ever you and your man decide to wear, give that costume a personality - seductive or silly. Get on your knees and give your man head in a security officer snap down shirt, hat and whip - get into character. Don't let him cume from that, but instead, stand in front of him with authority. Snatch your shirt open and sit on the edge of the bed with your legs opened wide and your sweet moist pussy exposed and ready to be sucked. Take your whip, point to him then take the whip and pat your lil pussy and say "get on your knees, it's your turn!" Betcha he won't be laughing at you. The

Chapter 9   **The Change**

both of you will never forget it and you can cume from this, too.
Props: Sex toys, foods, condiments and your favorite DVDs.

Just Have Fun

Setting up the stage: If you are still uncomfortable about the DVD getting out, don't worry - you might get your own reality show or a career boost, because of it (lol). But if that's not what you want, simply put a sheer piece of material over the lens as it records. Play around with the type of material. Iridescent materials, colored plastics, organza and laces might do the trick. You can also have the colored bulbs to make everything dim. You can use bright lights aimed at the lens to make it so bright that the glare distorts how you look, also.

The camera can just be focused on a specific part of the room or you can have the camera on part of the TV as it plays your favorite XXX rated DVD and shows just your bodies in motion in the glare of the TV. You can simply make a movie with your entire bodies in it or make a reality video and take the camera with you and the other person holds it while being pleasured by the other. Your goal is to have fun sexually and you will be better at giving oral because the both of you are doing something fun together. The arousal part in this is not just looking at what you've made but reminiscing about how you made it.

Step Out of Your Box

Voice overs and editing - (Optional) This video can actually be a fun project where one can do all the editing or you can do it separately and come together and show your work to one another. **BAM!** Two more oral and lovemaking sessions you can have watching your own movies. Although a XXX rated DVD seems like it would take hours to edit, it won't. The DVD you watch has been edited with extension clips to make it seem like they've been going at it for hours. NOT! If you and your man are average lovemaking people, a ½ hour is all you'll need from clothes off to snoring in the bed. If you know each other's bodies, cut that time in half. If you don't give head as often as your man needs and wants it, consider yourself below average. The goal is to change that *below* average and accelerate to the both of you being able to cume within 20 minutes (10 minutes each) from oral or lovemaking.

Remember, it doesn't take long to cume when you can tell a person what you need from them in order to be able to cume. You and your man will have a much better relationship when the two of you know each other sexually.

> Some of this might sound repetitive, but sometimes you need to hear or read something more than once on a different page or another day in order for you to **Just Get It!**

Chapter 9   **The Change**

HALT

Use your village of friends and family. If don't have a village, you must create one.

Choose your words wisely

If the words you chose to describe what you think of when you envision your man's penis or swallowing is negative and nasty to you, that will handicap you when it comes to the ultimate act of pleasing him.

Step Out of Your Box

Your Checklist

You need these items/the information to do the assignments and an open mind in order to complete the next couple of Assignments/Homework

 Cell phone with texting option

 Know the time you will be able to talk to him

 The time you will be see him

 A mental list of 4 of your favorite desserts and what you like about them (it)

 Love Supplies: Lubes, Good Head, D.T Spray, Mini vibe, Condoms (if you use them already), Toppings of choice-don't need all at once.

Chapter 9   **The Change**

Homework:
IT'S Time... Step OUT of the BOX

If you have not built up enough confidence to say what you feel, you can text this to him in three parts throughout the day until he comes home. Text what's below

1. I am sitting here thinking about how much I love you and I can't wait to lick your <u>sexy lips</u> and… (wait for him to respond or text #2 five minutes after #1)

2. I want to put my mouth on that *<u>big juicy polish</u>* in your pants... (wait for a response to text #2, then text #3 in five minutes if no response)

3. I want to feel your <u>creamy goodness</u> on my lips as I open up my mouth and mmmmm you finish the story when you cume home…

<u>**Use your own ego building and mouthwatering words for the underlined portions**</u>.

Proceed with caution. Telling a brotha the above can cause speeding, time loss from work or make him late for work; so make sure he is at work before you text or say these things. Also, be aware you'll get a much better response if you are not interfering with his sports or whatever he might be routinely into.

Help motivate others by emailing your/his reaction/story of your erotic text
www.villagesistagirlfriend.com
<u>Under Forum</u> (or email TEXT Reaction)

Step Out of Your Box

The Village Sista Girlfriend *Series*

You GO Girl!

YOU DID IT!

I am so proud of you. I hope you did all the assignments and homework. Most importantly, I hope your mind has been opened and the process of deprogramming yourself, in regards, to oral sex and loving your man has begun and soon be completely conquered.

Love
Annjee Mz. Jee's Spot

You are ready for the Next STEP.
Classes! Filled with fun and education
go to www.VSGseries.com (708) 868-4122
For details Or Scan below

Chapter 9   **The Change**

I hope this information has helped you in this minor dilemma.
If you are still in need of some motivation, then book your party.
www.VSGseries.com

Facebook: Village Sista Girlfriend or V.S.G.

Thank You

If you need a quick recap, go to the next page.
If you still have concerns or need to write something down for motivation, then go to
The Goal Page 204
And Get IT Done!!!

I need you to pass the word

Tell everyone about **V.S.G.**
I would love to give advice/speak about Relationships and other Topics
<u>On ANY media</u>
Call me for your next event

Thank You For
Your Support

Various products, classes and additional books coming soon

Table of Content

I hope you have read the book completely and have completed all the assignments. The Table of Content is in the back because this should be used as a reference for you to go to Chapters to review for conformation.

Chapter 1	WHY ME... Conflicted	P. 1-26
Chapter 2	I Can't Because... Fixable Dilemmas and Solutions	P. 27-96
Chapter 3	You Can Do This Self Help	P. 97-114
Chapter 4	OOOH! The Benefits of Giving Head	P. 115-122
Chapter 5	Anatomy of Your Man	P. 123-128
Chapter 6	The Sticky ickey of Things	P. 129-136
Chapter 7	The Gray Area Tips and Techniques Creating A New You	P. 137-178
Chapter 8	Lets GET IT Crackin Lights, Camera, Action	P. 179-188
Chapter 9	The Change Step Out of Your Box	P. 189-199
Resources	Scan and Share this information with friends	P. 200-204

WWW.VSGseries.COM
Love/Relationship Specialist - Mz. Jee's Spot

Chapter 9   **The Change**

Small Steps equals Big Success
NOT Forbidden

Confession Page

What do you feel you can do differently now?

What are you concerns?

What are your oral goals?

_____
_____
_____
_____
_____
_____
_____
_____
_____
_____

If you still need help, call, we are in the process of having sex education classes for ladies and couples?

Assignment/Homework

Goal Page

Write down what you will do differently now. Make it a part of your relationship... follow thru... You will do GREAT!!

_____
_____
_____
_____
_____
_____
_____
_____
_____
_____
_____
_____
_____
_____
_____
_____
_____
_____
_____
_____
_____

If you still need help, call, we are in the process of having sex education classes for ladies and couples?

Chapter 9   **The Change**

NOT Forbidden

Step UP Your Love Game - Call, and I will tell you how

Oral, Ladies Hen and Couples
Classes *are now available*

For the woman who want to step up her love game but need encouraging words, seriously fun education, training, laughter and a lil bit of our

Oral Be the Best BootCamp class starts NOW

Have Your Ultimate Hen Party
Finally Stress Free Fun for Ladies

Couples BootCamp

Talk to your Specialist or go online
for class information

Step Out of Your Box

Thank YOU - Share this information

AWESOME Book and Class Specials for the Village

Scan to see savings and details share this with friends

OR call (708) 868-4122

Support the Village, ask for the book at book stores, promote the parties and classes

FREE BOOK
Do you know of ladies (sistas) who are in need of this book and the message... Like NOW. You can help your girl out cheaply. Pass the book out as gifts with this great offer. Call or go to site> click *Book Specials* for the details

Get READY for Love & Deprogramming CLASSES You (The Host) get a FREE KIT with a Class OR a Free Gift when Hosting a party. Call or go to site> click *Book Specials* for the details

Become a STAR... Get a FREE Gift nd U can b ntered n 2 our raffle Call or go 2 site> click *Book Specials* for th details... It's a Face Book and Tweeter thing... Join Us!

SCAN for Deals on Books, Parties and Classes

www.ingramcontent.com/pod-product-compliance
Lightning Source LLC
Chambersburg PA
CBHW060514100426
42743CB00009B/1309